Father, Son and Brother Ghost

A Memoir

John MacKenna

The Harvest Press

Father, Son and Brother Ghost
John MacKenna
First published in 2024
by The Harvest Press.
www.theharvestpress.ie

ISBN 978-1-8380836-6-3

A Note on the Author

John MacKenna is the author of twenty-four books – novels, short-story collections, memoir, poetry and a biography – and a number of stage and radio plays. He is a winner of *The Irish Times*, Hennessy and Cecil Day-Lewis Awards. He is also a winner of a Jacob's Radio award for his documentary series on Leonard Cohen and a Worldplay Silver Medal (New York) for his radio play *The Woman at the Window* (RTE Radio 1). He teaches creative writing at Maynooth University and at The Hedge School on the Moone.

Also by John MacKenna

Novels
Clare
The Last Fine Summer
A Haunted Heart
The Space Between Us
Joseph
Hold Me Now

Short-Story Collections
The Fallen and Other Stories
A Year of Our Lives
The River Field
Once We Sang Like Other Men
We Seldom Talk About the Past

Memoir
Things You Should Know
Absent Friend

Non-Fiction
Castledermot and Kilkea: A Social History
Shackleton: An Irishman in Antarctica (with Jonathan Shackleton)
The Lost Village
I Knew This Place (Radio Essays)

Children's Books
Turkey's Delight
South

Poetry Collections
The Occasional Optimist
Ten Poems
Where Sadness Begins
By the Light of Four Moons

Plays
The Fallen
Who by Fire
The Unclouded Day
Towards Evening
Faint Voices
Sergeant Pepper
Over the Rainbow
The Woman at the Window
My Father's Life
Redemption Song
Lucinda Sly
Between Your Love and Mine (with Leonard Cohen)
The Mental

For

Dolores MacKenna

and

i.m. Una, Jack and Jarlath MacKenna

Maybe it's better there on the other side,
I hope that it is, for my sake and for his.

He should have known better than flying so close to the sun,
the wings couldn't hold, but he never did what he was told.

And Icarus fell while no one was looking,
we had places to go, and what could we do,
he fell out of the sky and disappeared in the blue forever.

I could have saved him, I could have, just one minute more,
had I thought of it then, but you know how it's been,
all this thinking I do lately takes all of my attention.

from *Icarus* – Krista Detor

Son

Sometimes we become the people our parents make of us.

Father

An evening in summer, sometime in the early 1990s, I called to visit my father. And there he was, standing at the foot of his tilled garden, leaning on the handle of a fork that was buried in the ground between two drills. I stood at the top of the garden, in the deep shadow of the garage, and watched him. It was so unusual to see him in that position – not working, absorbed in a world of his own. It was a warm evening and the sun still hadn't dipped beneath the western tree line. It cast a long shadow from my father's figure, a shadow that stretched back over eight decades.

We're a railway family, following the permanent way to wherever the next appointment takes us. It's 1908 and we're living in Ballybrophy when the youngest child, Jack, is born. And, soon afterwards, we're on the move again, this time to Carlow and Bluebell Cottage, where the five children and their parents settle into a new life.

The small boy, who is Jack, who is me, watches as the trains clatter by the end of the cottage garden, the colossal engines leaving trails of steam in the late spring sky. Inside the cottage, my mother, Kate, is fighting for her life. The year is 1910. My older brothers and sisters are warned not to say anything about our mother's illness to the toddler in the garden. Our father, Thomas, goes on working because he has to, doing what he can for his wife. The neighbours come and go. In the early summer Kate dies and shortly afterwards my siblings and myself are taken to Celbridge, to our maternal grandmother's house, while our father moves into lodgings in Carlow. Bluebell Cottage becomes a memory.

This new house where we live is crowded. My grandmother is a midwife but she shares her home with my aunt, my two cousins and us five, motherless children. Life is hard. I have no idea where my mother has gone. I will never know exactly where she is buried. Sometimes I imagine I remember a woman who looks a little like my aunt, a tall and graceful lady who sat me on her lap, who sang to me, who held me close when I was sick, who rocked me off to sleep on a long summer evening – but I can't be sure.

I try not to think too much; thoughts bring memories, memories bring sadness. Instead, I muddle on with my life. I start school, I make my First Communion and then word comes, when I'm eight or nine, word that the family is moving again. Back to be with our father in a town called Athy.

We travel to a cottage beside the railway tracks. The shadows of the trains block out the light as they pass. And one day my father introduces me to a woman called Julia Donohue, from County Clare. She's to be my new mother. I'm joyful beyond words.

But then the sadness comes again. Julia Donohue disappears. Died far too young, I hear a neighbour say as I'm lying in bed in the boys' room. The house falls silent. I wonder whether we will all move back again to our grandmother's house in Celbridge. Instead, my father tells me that my older sister, Lal, will look after us now. She's thirteen and she'll be in charge. I listen and I nod. I hope that Lal won't die.

I go to school to the Christian Brothers in Athy. The country is in the depths of war. I get involved in Fianna Eireann, I become a messenger. Sometimes when I'm carrying notes, I worry about being caught. Once, as I'm carrying a stolen gun from one side of the town to the other, I think about dying. I wonder what it's like to die, to be dead. I try to remember how my mother looked when she was dead but I can't remember her at all. I think of Julia Donohue in her coffin and I shiver. Crossing the Barrow Bridge I pass two Auxiliaries but they pay me no attention.

I go on to secondary school with the Christian Brothers' and when I finish I join the railway – just as my brother Michael has already done. But I'm restless. I know there must be more to the world. I go to England, work on the railways there, then come back home and join my father once again, working the permanent way.

In the late 1930s, I meet Una Bray at a dance. She's a teacher and she's beautiful and intelligent and full of life. She tells me she was born in Sligo but grew up in Tuam, County Galway, where her father was a train driver. We share an interest in politics and books and tennis and, in 1938, we become engaged. We marry in Castledermot, Co Kildare in 1940.

She often asks me about my early childhood but I can never find the answers to her questions and, when I try, the words come only in half sentences, unfinished stories. I seldom want to talk about the past.

We rent a house on Abbey Street in Castledermot and then we move into a County Council cottage in Abbeylands, the Low Terrace. Una teaches in the village school, I cycle to work in Athy. We have children, some living and some dead. I bury several stillborn children at the foot of our acre of garden. I never talk about the lost children, the children at the bottom of the garden, just as I never talk about my lost mothers.

Three children survive – Jarlath, Dolores and John. The family moves again, to a bigger house across the field, to the High Terrace. Sometimes the children ask me about my childhood. I fob them off with stories about the War of Independence. Once or twice, as we drive past Bluebell Cottage in Carlow, I nod and say, 'I lived there once,' but never more than that.

Brother Ghost

The sadness I feel – the longing for July and poppies and a bicycle and the freedom of teenage years to pick up speed down the long run from Mullaghcreelan to Kilkea bridge, the ache that is never quite gone, the moment that can never be recaptured – is that grief I feel at your death and my loss, a sadness resurrected now because you're almost twenty years gone and these rounded turning points seem to cry out, in living and dying, for something special, some celebration or observance. And, of course, I'm well past the age you were when you received the news. Yes, this sorrow has lost some of the awful bleakness of those earlier days and years but its core remains, rock solid, black, unmoving. It's the knot in my belly; the gloomy shadow in the garden; the dark place on the turn of the stairs; the longed-for ghost who almost appears but never quite comes into view. It's the constant, pitched hole in the sky at night and the sun's hesitation about rising at dawn.

And so, I sit down again to try to write something that will make sense of the lives we lived together, though it can never make sense of the death that pushed us apart. Not that words are of any practical use when it comes to pain, that pain that moves from my head to my soul, from my heart to my gut, that pain that is always there and always just beyond scrutiny, like an intermittent fault I can never quite pin down.

I have tried so often to put this feeling, these stories into words. I have given the grief two decades to condense but still it remains.

The loss is the pain; the emotional amputation goes on aching. The loss of that great sharing that is more than sharing, that is in the blood and of the blood – that tearing apart of the oneness that was and is our brotherhood.

Sometimes, it feels like a wonderful and generous gift, this pain that hasn't gone away. It's almost like you haven't gone away either and I just haven't worked out how to fully sense you or make sense of your presence. You disappear; I think you're gone for ever. I'm not sure what to make of that disappearance. And then I have a sensation of your being here again, a will o' the wisp outside the gate, beyond the window, among the apple trees, somewhere.

Mostly now you come in dreams. The other night I dreamt you and Clare arrived here with your children – in the dream they were still children. In the dream, I was in bed when you arrived – nothing new in that, I hear you laugh. It was very early morning and you'd just come off a flight from the States and driven from Dublin airport. You all came up to the bedroom to say hello and Clare and the children piled in but you stood in the doorway, smiling but distant. Later, we were in the garden. I was showing the children what I'd sown and what was growing, they were moving between the rows of beans and peas, stepping between the potato drills, the white potato blossoms brushing their tanned legs. Clare was moving behind them, saying: *Be careful you guys, don't trample Uncle John's plants* and we were all laughing. You were standing at the other end of the lawn, smiling but remote, there but not. I suspect this is how it's always going to be.

So I begin to tell the stories I need to tell, assemble the facts and the memories. I reimagine the unfinished conversations, the things you needed to say, the things I wanted to hear. Not that any of this will make one iota of difference, not that anything either of us says will reach the other's ears, not that all the listening in the world will allow me to hear your voice again. Yet these are the things I have to say to the great void, the endless absence that you've become.

Son

It's sometime, way back then, and it's a Christmas Day. I'm riding high on Jarlath's shoulders; he's a horse, a rocket, a giant and he's been delegated to keep me from getting under our mother's feet. Whatever the reason, whatever the excuse, I fall from that great height. My shoulder is dislocated. Bedlam ensues. I'm carted off to hospital while he stays at home with Dolores, our sister.

Here's a photograph of the two of us together, leaning back against the bonnet of the black Ford Prefect. He has one arm around me; the other is draped across the shimmering headlight. In another picture he's sitting on the running-board of the car and I'm sitting on his lap. And here's one of the three of us on the swing in the back yard – steps of stairs. He's at the back, Dolores is in the middle and that's me at the front, bow-legged. I'm squinting into the early afternoon sun; my face has the seriousness of a small, pudgy bishop. Dolores is smiling, that spirit of optimism and possibility that she has carried with her through good days and bad already there. But Jarlath's eyes are downcast. Maybe it's the embarrassment of a twelve-year-old, corralled into a photograph when he'd much rather be elsewhere, doing the things he wants to do. But I have a sense that there's something happening, some inkling of a huge responsibility already weighing on his mind.

When I look at the earlier photographs there's a difference. Here's one taken on a picnic at Rice's Hill – he stands with the picnic bag on his nine-year-old arm, his smiling face open to the sun; Dolores is there, too, holding her doll aloft; our father is seated on a rock, wearing a three-piece suit. Or another one, another picnic, and Jarlath is goofing it up, a huge teacup covering half his face. An earlier one – he and our sister seated on the wing of a small aeroplane; she's about four so he must be eight. Our father is leaning against the fuselage, again in a three-piece suit. Earlier still, Jarlath is in a playpen outside the back door of the house in which we were born. He has a full head of curly hair. He's probably eighteen months old, still an only child and he wears that smile that will charm the birds off the trees.

Is it my imagination or are these early photographs saturated with light and laughter and possibility? It seems to me that his eyes are wide, his head is up, he is looking out at the future and it stands, off camera, like a promise, and he can't wait to be a part of it. That openness and optimism are there time after time – communion and confirmation, seaside holidays and afternoons in the garden.

But in this picture of the three of us, perched on the swing that, ironically, could have carried seven, his eyes are definitely downcast, the shadow has already fallen and I sense the weight of the immense world beginning to bear down on him.

There's one photograph that might have been the exception to my retrospective theory. It's the one that hangs above my desk and I'm looking at it now. We're sitting on the swing again, that sturdy contraption built with railway sleepers. Someone – he or Dolores – has chalked the words *A Party* on the upright. Behind us is the shed, like a Mexican adobe in the strong sun of a high summer day. The shadows are dark and definite in this picture. He's sitting on the right-hand side of the swing and I'm on the left. He's probably twelve years old and I'm about eighteen months. My legs are bowed, my boots are scuffed, I'm wearing a dribbler and my hair still has the high blond curls of infancy. I have a spoon in my right hand and there's a plate on the wooden seat. Jarlath is in short trousers and shirt, his socks bunched like a collapsed concertina and his shoes lost in the grass. He's smiling, we both are, but even here the shadows cast by the burning sun have darkened his eyes and it seems as though he's smiling in spite of, rather than because of, the summer day.

And then there's that afternoon at the Mill Pond, the deep, dark lake that sat beside the slow, shallow trickle of the river Lerr. No photographs of that. Someone had dammed the river years before, to make a small swimming pool, three feet deep and fifteen feet wide, a safe place for children to learn to swim. But the Mill Pond is another matter. Built to supply a run of water for the mill at Prumplestown, it has become a still and reputedly bottomless backwater where only those who can swim with confidence will venture. On that sunny afternoon in 1955, my brother and his friends bring me on an adventure to the Mill Pond. They also carry the large tin bath which is our mobile bathing vessel on Saturday nights, and a length of rope. I am to be the adventurer – set adrift on the Mill Pond in the tin bath, one end of the rope tied to a handle on the tub, the other held by one or other of my brother's friends. I must have maintained a cool head and my equilibrium because I survive. Our mother is away from home that day and our father is working, but I can't wait to tell them both of my great voyage when they get back in the evening. They're less than impressed and not particularly amused.

These are the days I don't clearly remember and these are the family stories that have travelled far, arriving like weatherworn spectres. But here they are – retold, embellished, turned on their heads like the falling child who was me. And always and forever, at the heart of the stories, are the three children, two boys and a girl, ten years between oldest and youngest, a sister between her brothers. He and she and I. Him and her and me. Us. We. Siblings. Family. Survivors of our own small carnage though we didn't know it back then.

When I try to imagine that time, I go back to the question – were we already carrying the weight of who and what we'd turn out to be; whether any of us sensed the plot of the shadow play our lives would finally become; whether we had any inkling of those we'd left behind? Did we have some shadowy suspicion that the falling leaves were to be the calendar of all our days to come? Or were we just getting on with our lives as others were getting on with theirs? Memory may be recovered but so many of the figures who peopled its shores are beyond reach now. Remembering becomes this bitter frustration, a trap that lures me in with promises of the past, only to betray with an overpowering sense of its uselessness, its lost and irredeemable detail. And, yet, after all, when it comes to him, memory is the only thing I have, the last tentative, remaining space where I can go to meet my brother.

Brother Ghost

I was seven and you were seventeen. We had moved into the new house, on the High Terrace, the previous summer and you came home from boarding school at Christmas, all agog. You talked incessantly about Tchaikovsky and his *1812 Overture*, you took us through it, note by note it seemed – the roar of the gunfire was what caught my attention – and how it begins with Russian tunes and moves on through the cannon shots and the *Marseillaise* and the Russian hymn while Moscow is laid waste and then the triumphant *God Save the Tzar* and even more cannon shots, all building to a memorable end. You did all this with such enthusiasm, with lightness in your voice, with delight at the knowledge you'd gathered and at the fact that you could share that knowledge. And you did it so well that we forgot that we didn't even have a record player at the time and had never heard the music.

'You'll make a great teacher,' our mother said and our father smiled. He wanted more for you than he had ever got and being a teacher would be a wonderful thing. I could be the railwayman.

Years later, Mozart became your muse, your music man. Yes, you still listened to the hits of the sixties; yes, you were still amused by the lyrics of Gilbert and Sullivan but Mozart was *the man*. You rhapsodised about his music down the phone; when we met, you reminded me that I should listen to his work; you played his music in your car while we drove; you and Clare took a trip to visit his burial place in Vienna and you sent me a photograph you'd taken there of a solitary red rose on his snow-covered grave.

I'm listening now to Mozart's inspirational and life-affirming melodies and I'm seeing you again: enthralled, your eyes ablaze, that wide, wild smile of yours, your face radiant as the music pours from the car speakers. Outside, the sun is blazing down on the roads of North Carolina. Inside, you turn the air-conditioning to full and the coldness sweeps over us and you tell me about the Viennese trip, about the cemetery, about Mozart and every now and then you say: 'Listen to this bit' and the music grows louder and swells till I think the car windows are about to burst. But you're alive and the miles of road and the acres of tobacco plants fly by us and the wide, calm sea comes into view and the music goes on pouring over us, washing us towards the warm ocean, coursing through the hot afternoon, lifting us forward, to brighter times, the narrow minds and dark days of sixties Ireland falling away behind us like the wreck of another, best forgotten life.

'Will you ever go back to Ireland?' I ask in the moment between movements.

You shake your head but you don't say anything for a long time. And when you do speak, the first movement of *Eine Kleine Nachtmusik* as your soundtrack, all you say is: 'I don't think so.'

I want to ask why. I want to ask if I'm correct in thinking you have no great love for the Ireland you left, that it's peopled with too many ghosts, that you feel as ill-at-ease there as I sometimes do. But something in the brevity of your reply makes me think better of it. And then Mozart's *Second Flute Concerto* is playing and the mood has changed and we drive in silence.

Years later, in the week after your death, I drove your car down these same roads and I flicked on the CD player, wondering about the music you had listened to on your last trip home from the beach. The music I heard was the hits of the fifties and sixties – Johnny Ray and Fats Domino and Buddy Holly and Little Richard and Elvis and the Beatles and the Chiffons and Skeeter Davis and the Beach Boys and Bobby Darin. No Mozart, no Gilbert and Sullivan, no Clancy Brothers – nothing to remind you of home or Europe or schooldays, just the songs that you chose to play on the last, long drive back from the shore to home. And while I listened, I feared I was beginning to lose the connection with you – for the first time ever, I felt I was listening to the music of a stranger and an iciness touched me, despite the heat of a full summer day outside.

By the time I was four you were in boarding school and then university and then gone to practice medicine in the States. But it's more than just the age difference that gave me this sense of understanding and dependency. It was my reliance on you, my trust in you, my knowing that once you were around I'd be safe. When you were home on holiday – less and less as you worked the college summers in England – I felt that the weight of the world was lifted off my shoulders. I was no longer the only child that I became when you and Dolores were away at school or college or working.

You must remember the two sheepdogs we had – Brandy and Soda, you named them after George Hobbs' show-jumper. Soda came by train from Mayo, a lean, nervous little fellow who grew into a warm-hearted, lean and nervous bigger fellow. In the meantime, while we were waiting for his arrival, I lost patience and brought home another sheepdog pup from Dinny Murphy's house. This fellow was short-legged, stout and rowdy – more confident than Soda. And yet the pair of them got along like a house on fire. *Whither thou goest, I will go.*

There was a time, when Soda was a pup – it must have been the end of a summer because you were just back from working in Wall's factory in England – that he came close to dying after he'd been poisoned. You stayed up all night for two nights to give him his medicine and watch over him. And for the following two nights you got up every hour to make sure he was doing alright. I remember you rolling out of bed, crossing the landing quietly and slipping downstairs to check on him. I'd turn over and go back to a half-sleep, and when you came upstairs I'd ask how he was.

'He's doing fine,' you'd say. 'He'll be alright. Now get some shut-eye.'

And he was.

Ironically, the dogs were both dead within a year of your leaving. Soda was poisoned again and Brandy bled to death after a fight with another dog.

I remember him creeping into the yard, blood clotted on the thick fur around his neck. He limped into the corral our father had built for him in the back of the garage, a place of warm straw. By the time I'd got inside to get a cloth and water to wash the wound and brought it out to the garage, he'd bled to death.

That was the same dark, warm space where Michael O'Neill and Liam Mulhall and Seán Healy and Olive Hunt and myself had our gang meetings. And that was the place I hid your copy of *Lolita*, after our mother had found it under your bed and ordered me to burn it on a bonfire at the bottom of the garden. But I couldn't burn this book – not because it was a *dirty book* but because it was a hardback and I'd seen hardback books used in spy films. The centres were hollowed out and used as hiding places for treasures. So, page by page, I hollowed out the centre of *Lolita* and Nabokov's masterpiece became the storage place for the treasures of our gang: a key, to what no one knew but we believed one day the mystery would be solved; a white stone found in Keatley's field; a rusty penknife that wouldn't open; three cigarette cards; half a large cigar and a fountain pen that leaked.

This was the hiding place where I deposited the *News of the World* on Sundays. You were the one who sent me into Mary Nolan's shop to buy it – we bought our regular Sunday papers in George Abbot's.

'Just do it,' you'd say, 'and I'll give you threepence.'

'Why don't *you* buy it?'

'I'm busy.'

'If Mammy finds out.'

'Well, she won't. Just leave it in the garage when you get back home.'

'Why do you buy the *News of the World*?'

'For the racing.'

And I believed you.

And then there were the football matches on the front lawn, played in the few days between your coming home from England and going back to college. End to end stuff, twenty goals the winner. I had speed, you had guile. I had boyish enthusiasm, you had the arguments. My prize, if I won, was something magical.

'If you win, I'll buy you a bike.'

And when I won it was doubles or quits, though what I'd do with two or four or eight bicycles I never knew. I loved those hours together on the lawn, our mother telling us to *be careful of the roses* and it never mattered that I was always the one sneaking into O'Connell's garden next door to delicately retrieve the ball from the midst of Mrs O'Connell's peony roses and delphiniums, propping up the broken stems in the hope that she wouldn't notice.

You left for America owing me a shed full of bikes but I didn't care. I didn't miss the bikes. I just missed you.

Son

And fifty years are gone like the swoop of a swallow.

It's an afternoon in the early summer of 1971 and my friend Pat Clowry and myself are standing on the roadside at Newlands Cross, ahead of the Friday evening hitch-hikers. I've skived off my last history lecture of the week, as I often do on a Friday, and, even though the exams are looming, needs must.

Pat and I are the Friday night DJs at the exotically named Trudeau's Discotheque in the old cinema in Castledermot. We each do a one hour set before the band takes to the stage. Getting on the Naas Road early means we've a good chance of making it home before tea-time, catching a lift or two before the single, female hitchers scupper our chances.

As we stand on the roadside, thumbs in the air, I turn to Pat: 'I want you to do something for me.'

'And that is?'

'When you're doing your set tonight, I want you to play "I am I said."'

'Come on,' Pat laughs. 'Me, play Neil Diamond? That would be my credibility tattered in three minutes.'

His set is normally filled with Van Morrison, Neil Young, The Doors and Led Zeppelin. Neil Diamond is definitely not cool.

'Listen,' I say, naming a young woman we both know, 'she'll be there and I want to ask her to dance and that's a good song, I think it'll help, it's got all that existential angst and a bloody good tune. Play just that one song, tag it on to your "Crazy Love" and "Only Love Can Break Your Heart" set. I'll even buy you a buidéal oráiste for your inner páiste.'

This is the kind of slick exchange that seems hip at Newlands Cross in 1971.

'And I'll finish my set ten minutes early,' I offer. 'Give you seventy minutes before the band comes on.'

That is the clincher.

'Alright but never again!' Pat says and, with that, a lorry slows and stops.

'Where are you pair heading?' the driver asks.

'The centre of the universe. Castledermot.'

'Hop in.'

And we're on our way.

Seven hours later, in the soft wash of the disco lights, a slow set begins with "Crazy Love" and I cross the floor and pop the question: 'Would you like to dance?'

The answer is non-committal, a shrug, a glance at the friends and a measured, uncertain saunter onto the crowded floor.

While we move slowly to the rhythm, I try to make conversation but the initial replies to my questions are monosyllabic. Yes. No. D'no.

However, by the time Van Morrison has finally gone crazy and Neil Young has had his heart broken and the opening chords of the Neil Diamond song are ringing round the disco, I have established, I feel, some kind of rapport. The answers to my questions have become multi-syllabic and I'm even asked what I'm studying in UCD. And then a comfortable silence falls between us and the young woman seems to relax into my arms.

It's on the second chorus of the song that I make my monumental blunder. As Neil Diamond sings: 'I am, I said, to no one there, and no one heard at all, not even the chair…' I join in without realising I'm singing.

The young woman steps back, holding me at arms-length.

'Are you talking about me?' she asks.

'No, no, God no,' I stammer. 'I just like the song, the lyrics are good.'

She shakes her head slowly and remains at a very, very unsocial distance until the music fades.

'Would you like to stay on for the next set?' I ask.

She looks me straight in the eyes. I imagine the slowly strobing lights weaving their romantic spell between us and then she speaks, very softly and very sincerely: 'Did you ever read about a frog who dreamed of being a king but never became one?' she asks. 'Because, except for the names and a few other changes, you'll always remain one.' And, with that, she's gone through the mill of dancers, back to her friends in the seats to the side of the dance floor.

I stand there for a moment and then glance up at Pat, behind the turntables. He shrugs his shoulders as if to say, 'I did my best for you,' and then he mimes to me that the long promised bottle of orange would be welcome and I make my way to the mineral-bar, Neil Diamond's words still ringing in my head and I am lost and I can't even say why.

And, by the time I turn to look again at the dance floor, the place is empty and fifty years have passed like the swoop of a swallow.

Father

When I was in primary school, in Athy, the ten mile drive home, after my father had finished work, was often silent. But sometimes my father would talk about the railway. He had worked on the railway for most of his life; his father and brother had worked on the railway and my mother's father and brother had worked on the railway. We were a railway family.

By then, my brother was studying medicine and my sister was on her way to becoming a teacher. I was the last possible candidate to take my grandfathers', uncles' and father's places with CIE.

My father would assure me that, with a good Leaving Certificate, I could expect to go far in the company.

'You could work your way up to Station Master and Inspector.' Inspector was the highest accolade my father could imagine. That would be the top of the tree as far as he was concerned.

'It's a good career and steady. And for a chap like you, with a head on his shoulders, the sky's the limit. If you got a good Leaving Cert you'd have all the options open to you. It's something you should think about.'

At the time, I just wanted to work on the trains. The idea of being stuck in an office held no appeal for an eleven-year-old. Better still, I could be a guard on a goods' train. The guard's van seemed like heaven to me, with its wood-burning stove and burnt-black kettle; the hard wooden bunks; the sandwiches wrapped in newspaper; the door opening onto a platform at the rear; the steep steps down; the red and green oil-burning lanterns on the back. It offered everything a boy could want – freedom, privacy, travel, adventure, responsibility. I had visions of long trips from Dublin to Sligo – the stove burning brightly and the kettle singing while the wind and rain stormed outside. At home, I took over a disused rabbit hutch, hung sacks over the open sides and pretended it was a guard's van. If ever I worked on the railway, I decided, I wanted to be a guard.

'You'd soon grow tired of that,' my father would say but I didn't believe him. Who could grow tired of such an escapade? New stations, new people but, most importantly, the solitude in between. I didn't know the word solitude back then, I only knew the word aloneness but it was that aloneness that appealed to me.

I was never happier than when I was out walking the dogs, Brandy and Soda, over Rice's Hill, down through the Rocks and out past Halfmiletown. Out there the countryside was deserted – just me and the dogs and my imagination. I dreamt of living in Joe Shea's derelict cottage on the banks of the river Lerr. I spent summer days walking and imagining. Later, in my teens, I walked and imagined and hoped I'd meet some Ruth in search of her Boaz but all I saw was the occasional fisherman, as anxious to avoid me as I was to avoid him.

'Sure, have a think about it,' my father would say, as we pulled into the yard at home.

'I will,' I'd say.

Years afterwards, when I was in my thirties, I realised that my father wasn't just interested in seeing me settled in a permanent and pensionable job with prospects. He loved the idea of the family continuing its connection with the railways. His own career had been thwarted as a result of his involvement in a strike, and his ambition of becoming a Station Master or an Inspector had never been achieved. His job as foreman in Athy railway station was important to him, and he valued the position, but there was within him that *might have been*, that knowledge that he was intelligent enough and ambitious enough to have made it farther up the ladder. Despite his night-school studies, he believed, his active union involvement with the National Association of Transport Employees had stood in his way. I think he saw in me the chance for the family to make an even bigger mark in CIE, the national railway company. But I was to disappoint him and, despite a summer spent working on the permanent way, teaching, my mother's trade, became mine, too, if only for a time. But the allure of the guard's van never faded, even when the vans themselves disappeared.

Son

Heaven help our innocence. We're out on the football field, the old football field, at the back of Abbeylands, the field that will – in time – become a development of new houses but is, for now, our place of recreation and wildness.

There are six of us – Joe Whelan; two of the Hickeys; Liam Mulhall; Michael O'Neill and myself. We've been playing Gaelic football for twenty minutes and then someone suggests we play soccer. This is 1960, the month is June and Wolves have recently won the FA Cup, beating Blackburn 3 – 0. Spurs are the league champions and Chelsea – which will become *my* team in a year or two – is unknown to me. But one of the lads has heard about the FA Cup from a cousin, who saw it on TV in another cousin's house in Dublin, and he gives us a rundown on his version of the rules and off we go, three against three. The football posts make one goal, two jumpers on the twenty-one yard line make the other.

But, within minutes, the game is in uproar. A high ball comes in and the goalkeeper catches it.

'Penalty,' someone shouts.

'For what?' the keeper asks.

'You handled the ball.'

'Yeah. So?'

'The goalie isn't allowed to handle the ball in soccer.'

'Course he is.'

'No, he's not. No one can handle the ball in soccer.'

'So how am I supposed to stop it?' the hapless keeper asks.

'With your legs or your body.'

'Or your head,' someone else laughs. 'It's thick enough!'

The argument goes on. Some of us believe the keeper is allowed to handle the ball and some believe he isn't. The truth is: nobody knows for sure.

'Why don't we go back to football?' the goalkeeper asks.

'We might as well. It makes way more sense than this shite.'

Father

This is how it was or this is how I remember it. The autumn of 1964. My mother's birthday was coming up and things were not good at home. There'd been weeks of bickering and arguing between my parents. Maybe it was worse for me than it was for them, maybe they'd become accustomed to each other's sniping. But, mostly, it was down to alcohol and its power to rip relationships apart and drive people to their wits' end. At this remove, it's a haze. One bout of arguing and shouting and door-slamming and silence blurs into another but the sense of disquiet remains. It's as easy to tap into that time and that unease from sixty years away as it is to step outside the door.

The only thing that has changed is that those same years have stilled my parents' voices, laid them side by side in the quiet of the graveyard in Coltstown, outside Castledermot.

I remember dropping hints about my mother's birthday, on the journeys to and from school. Whether my father wasn't listening or wasn't hearing I don't know. I know he wasn't one for celebrating birthdays. Perhaps it went back to his own wretched childhood, to all the absences that marked that early time in his life. Not surprising, then, that he saw Christmas as *a sad old time* or that the sentiment of birthdays was simply sentimentality to him. But, at eleven years of age, I knew none of this and no one thought to tell me. Why should they? I was just a child and how could I understand the kinds of things the grown-ups in the house didn't understand themselves?

Two days before my mother's birthday, I stole a half-crown from her purse. That afternoon, when school was over, I took my courage in my hand and walked into the record shop in Athy and bought her a copy of Jim Reeves "I Won't Forget You." And then I took what was left of my courage and told my Aunt Lal, my father's sister, that it was my mother's birthday on that day. When my father came to collect me after work, my aunt produced a pair of stockings – their packaging slightly damaged – and gave them to my father to give as a birthday present to my mother.

I know – I know well – that for many men and women of my father's generation, and for my father in particular, the warmth, the particular joy and the celebration of a birthday were foreign. I remind myself now that he was shunted from Billy to Jack in his childhood; that he grew up in a house where birthdays were a luxury that could not be afforded financially or emotionally. But on that evening in the autumn of 1964 I knew none of this.

It was then, as it is now, as though I were standing outside myself and the situation, watching. I saw a small boy bringing home a record to his mother for her birthday, bought with money stolen from her purse, and a man bringing a last minute gift, wrapped in a brown paper bag from my uncle's shop, to his wife. Even now, it's a moment that sneers at me at the least opportunity.

Son

I'm in fifth class in primary school. My mother has a passion for the Irish language and she reckons my Irish is far from *snasta*. And so I'm sent to the Connemara Gaeltacht, to the village of Tír an Fhiadh, for three months – from January to March of that year. Mind you, I'm not the only one to hit the road west – two or three girls from my village are also sent packing to brush up on the *blas*, but we're settled in houses far from each other, no chance of our keeping in touch or speaking *as Bearla* to one another.

We all land in neighbouring townlands and are deposited in houses where we go through a process of total immersion in the language. My house has a wonderful and endlessly talkative *bean a tí*; and a *fear a' tí* who says very little but smiles a lot, and two small boys, aged three and five. It doesn't have electricity or running water but it has a really warm welcome and the house next door seems to have an endless rota of children in and around my own age and they, too, make me welcome and help me overcome my homesickness.

Not only do these neighbours have electricity in their home, they also have a television, which is more than we have at home, and a place is made for me on the extended settee – which is in fact a brilliantly devised series of car seats which can be added to or subtracted from as the audience demands. Where the cars have gone I'll never discover. Of course, I'm not supposed to watch television because the programmes are in English but, as my *bean a' tí* is fond of saying: *Níl aon dochar ann.*

The only danger to my surreptitious and harmless television-watching – which stretches to half an hour, twice a week – is the local *Ceannaire*, the man on the bike who can (and does) call unannounced to ensure we're not speaking English, watching television or getting up to any other kinds of devilment. Sometimes he arrives at the school and each *dalta* is taken out to the corridor for a quick pep talk and an interrogation. Sometimes, he arrives at the house and drinks tea and eats bread and jam and talks about me as though I'm not there and, sometimes, I meet him on the road or in the village and he stops to ask gruffly if my Irish is improving.

In the second week of February 1964 a wave of excitement washes over the house next door. Word has leaked out that there's to be a film in the local *halla* on the following Friday night and all the children aged ten and over are going and won't I come too and won't we all have a wonderful time and isn't this the best thing ever?

Ar agaidh leat, the bean a' tí says, *sure nach bhfuil na lads next door ag dul fresin*? The *fear a' tí*, as ever, says nothing at all, just nods and smiles.

And so it comes to pass – Wednesday drifts into Thursday and Thursday into Friday and the excitement is monumental. I go to the *siopa* that afternoon, on my way from school, and spend my week's pocket money – all but the admission price – on sweets for all of us. By tea-time we're like hens on a hot griddle and by seven o'clock we're ready to leave, giving ourselves an hour to make the five-minute walk.

We get there in the end, thirty minutes before the film is due to begin, take our seats in the front row and I share the sweets with my companions. Bit by bit the *halla* fills and by ten to eight the place is packed. If the lights go down now and the film starts none of what is about to happen next might ever have occurred, but the lights don't go out and, somehow or other, the *Ceannaire* sees me among the children in the front row. Not that I'm hiding – as far as I'm concerned there's no reason to hide. But he has other ideas.

He stomps up the aisle, lifts me by the arm from my seat, my sweets scattering across the floor.

Tá bloody hard neck agat teacht isteach anseo, is all he says but his voice booms through the quietened hall as he frog-marches me to the door and pushes me into the darkness outside.

I hang around for a while, humiliated and afraid but, in the end, the cold drives me home to my lodgings. Too embarrassed to tell the truth, I say I don't feel well. The *bean a' tí* makes hot milk and toast and tucks me into bed.

The following morning, the oldest of the girls from the house next door – she's probably fourteen or fifteen – arrives with my scattered sweets intact and with the truth about what happened the night before.

The *fear a' tí* listens, as ever, in silence and then says, very quietly: *Ná bach leis an bpleidche sin, nil ann ach fear beag ar rothar mór*. (Don't mind that fool, he's nothing but a small man on a big bike.)

I may not understand the subtleties in what he says but I get the gist and I feel a damn sight better.

Brother Ghost

A lot of the time, I was lonely in Tír an Fhiadh. You knew that because I told you. I was lonely and I was frightened, despite the fact that the house in which I was staying could not have been more welcoming, the young couple and their two small boys couldn't have made me feel more at home. There might have been no running water, no bathroom, no electricity, but in the February the couple loaned me their transistor radio and alarm clock so that I could listen to the Sonny Liston/Cassius Clay World Heavyweight title fight in the small hours. And the family next door, the O'Conghailí, had that television which I watched, despite the *Ceannaire*'s dire warnings of expulsion. They, too, were warm, welcoming and couldn't have done more to make my stay enjoyable. But Tír an Fhiadh wasn't home and my great fear was that I had no idea what was happening at home. I had left a house where bickering and arguing and silences had become the norm.

Sometime in that three-month stay the weekly letter from home didn't arrive and then a second week passed without a missive and my imagination got to work. It didn't cross my mind that our mother might be up to her eyes with other things.

I wrote to you, an epistle filled with panic. You knew how things at home were often fraught, I said, though the language I used was simpler. There might have been a row. Our mother might have left and gone away. I might never see her again.

I remember walking to the Post Office, buying the stamp, checking that I had the address of your digs in Cabra correctly spelled, then posting the letter and beginning the wait for a reply. I don't know whether you spoke to them at home or whether it was coincidence but, by the end of the week, you'd written back to say all was ok; a letter had come from our mother with a postal order for five shillings and Clare, your girlfriend, had written to me, enclosing some comics and a crepe-paper Tipperary hat, one of those hats sold outside football and hurling matches, the ones that ran in the rain and left the wearer with a multi-coloured face. I breathed again.

And Monday after Monday, from then on, a *Beano* and a *Dandy* arrived from Clare and the letters from home resumed and I grew to accept, if not to like, my fate. Did you pass on the responsibility for keeping in touch to Clare? Most likely you did. Back then, you never took those things as seriously as I did. Perhaps you were the wiser man.

Son

How to describe the indescribable? A promise of light in the window, edging beneath the curtain. I look across at the other bed in our room, the lads' room. My brother is fast asleep. I slip into the frosty air and follow the wedge of brightness from the landing light. Down the stairs, stopping at the foot, in the glow from the Christmas candle that has burned all night in the hall window. Waiting. Listening.

What if he's still there? What if I open the sitting room door and he's still there, taking the presents from his sack? What if he turns to face me, the slice of cake that I left for him half in and half out of his mouth? What if the glass of milk is raised to his lips as I poke my head around the door?

I sit on the bottom step of the stairs for a moment, listening, trying to ignore the breathing of the sleepers above me, tuning my ears to the downstairs silence. No sound. I have no idea what time it is but I venture on, across the hall, turning the squeaky knob on the sitting room door. Pausing. Pushing. Stepping after it into the soft flush of the Christmas tree lights.

And there they are. The presents on the floor near the fire grate and, beside them, the empty glass and plate with its relics of crumbs that have fallen from Santa's lips. To be so close to his presence, to touch the glass and the plate he had touched, as close to the dream as the dreamer can come. I had far more faith in the truth of those fallen crumbs than I had in the transubstantiated hosts of Sunday mornings.

And afterwards the toys, the books, the sweets. I eat and play and read and eat and play and fall asleep on the couch. And, when I wake again, daylight is drenching the window panes and the fire is lighting in the grate and someone has draped a blanket over me and the family is busy in the kitchen.

This is Christmas day. *Christus natus est.*

Father

The weeks and days leading to Christmas were always busy in our house. The beet season meant late working hours for my father as the trains, loaded for Carlow sugar factory, travelled at all hours of the day and night. Preparations for school concerts and plays saw my mother working long past school closing hours. Christmas cards arrived and were sent but my father never seemed to have time to read the incoming communications which were put on the bookshelves and on strings across the sitting room walls.

Finally, on December 25th, in the quiet hours after Christmas dinner, he would work his way methodically through the cards, taking them down, reading the messages and verses, passing the odd comment, before returning them to their places.

There was something comforting in that tradition, a promise that all might be well with the world in the coming year. I'd leave the house, taking the dogs across the late afternoon fields, stopping to look at the Christmas tree lights in our sitting-room window, at the candle burning in the hall window, knowing that – for now – all was well with the world. I imagined the scene inside. My brother reading, my sister and mother watching a film on television and my father working his way through the Christmas post, the fire blazing, the unopened presents beneath the tree – to be unwrapped on my return. This was how life could be – peaceful, wonderful, calm and comforting.

Son

My sister, Dolores, reminds me that I was raised as an Irish speaker by our mother.

Whenever Dolores took the toddler me down to the village people would stop us and ask her to get me to say something in Irish.

In the butcher's shop I had no hesitation in asking for *feoil* and then eating the raw, red meat given me by Frank McDonald.

I wonder why I was the only one raised as an Irish speaker.

'I think she probably got tired of child-rearing and thought she'd try something different with you!' Dolores laughs.

And she reminds me that our mother was forty-seven when I was born.

'By the time you finished primary school she was almost sixty, her energy must have been running out.'

Brother Ghost

Stephen's Day – it was never St Stephen's Day – that day when I could have been out as a Wren boy but wasn't; that day when I should have gone with my friends to the matinee but didn't; that day when all of us might have had a lie-in, as you pointed out over breakfast, but couldn't. And all for the same good reason – the trip to Tuam, the annual pilgrimage from east to west; out of the sleeping village that was home; across the midlands in the Morris Minor from the back seat of which we'd glimpse *wran* boys and girls going about their own pilgrimage, house to house and door to door, gathering the goodies that they, no doubt, would share at the matinee in their local cinemas. Oh how I envied them.

On through dozing towns and villages, the streets still Christmas quiet, the curtains undrawn; the cats curled up like tea cosies on windows, waiting for the first signs of life; the milk bottles nesting on doorsteps; not a trickle of smoke from any chimney – and why would there be? It was still early morning.

We'd stop off in Moate and sit with the cousins in my aunt and uncle's kitchen, our parents drinking tea while I kept an eye on the half-open box of Black Magic at the edge of the couch, waiting for my aunt to make the offer I couldn't refuse. Then I'd stuff as many sweets into my mouth as possible – while you and Dolores frowned on my bad manners. But it was worse than that. By the time we'd crossed the bridge in Athlone, I could feel the sweets regurgitating, they moved and rumbled and shifted like an avalanche in my throat.

'Hang on,' my father said. 'Hang on till I find a gate.'

Then a quick exit and I reacquainted myself with the sweets. They came up whole.

'You didn't even chew them,' my mother sighed.

'Disgusting,' Dolores added as I climbed back in. I got a window seat this time – just in case.

A couple of miles down the road, you started to sing quietly.

'That old black magic has me in its spell.
that old black magic that you weave so well,
those icy fingers up and down my spine.'

'Enough!' my mother said and you fell silent, still smiling. The towns and villages passed. And the rain began to fall.

Tuam was as Tuam always seemed to be – wet, beneath a sky drenched with the smell of turf-smoke.

My grandmother had the table set and we sat in to a second Christmas dinner in two days. My mother warned me not to rush my food, you grinned and winked.

After the meal was over, the cousins and aunts and uncles materialized from the darkness outside and I found myself walking through the empty streets with the younger cousins, down to the only sweet shop that opened on Stephen's Day. The shopkeeper, a woman, was weeping loudly as she served us. Years later I would discover she had lost her young son in a Hallowe'en fire the previous autumn. We spent the money we'd been given then meandered back to our grandparents' house in Church View.

In the window the Christmas candle was lighting and, inside, the table was being readied for tea. This would be followed at half-nine or ten o'clock by 'a cuppa before ye go.'

Then it was back into the Morris Minor. The seats were cold, the car was cold, the heater it seemed ran on candle power but before we were well clear of the town, my mother started the rosary and by the time she reached the third Glorious Mystery, I was fast asleep. I'd come to now and then and mumble: 'Where are we?' and the word would come back from the front seat, Loughrea or Tullamore or Geashill, and I'd drop off again, dreaming of the *Wran* and the cinema and the matinee I'd missed.

Then, suddenly, I was awake. The car had stopped and you were lifting me onto your knee while Dolores made room on the narrow back seat. I could hear running feet. Outside the night was pitch-black. The car door opened and I saw the faces of two girls from Castledermot.

'Thanks very much,' one of them said.

They scrambled in, perching on the edge of the back seat. I could smell their perfume.

'We thought we'd have to walk all the way home,' the second girl said as the overloaded car pulled slowly away.

'Were ye in Dreamland?' my mother asked, naming the dancehall in Athy.

'We were.'

'And was it good?' my father wanted to know.

'The band was good. But that was it,' the first girl giggled and her soft voice and her laughter were an anaesthetic to me. And when I woke again, you were carrying me across the yard and through the dimly lit kitchen and then it was morning and I was in my own bed and Stephen's Day was over and the pilgrimage had been made for another year.

Son

If boarding school in a religious Juniorate is the number one way of preparing my brother and myself for the possibility of the priesthood then the round of religious observances at home comes a close second.

My mother is a regular Mass-goer – a daily Mass-goer during Lent – but it isn't just Mass that draws her to the church. Up until the end of fourth class – at which point a bad beating at the hands of one of my teachers sends me to the Christian Brothers school in Athy where, ironically, I will be slapped only once – I go every afternoon with my mother to the local church to make the stations of the cross. I race around the fourteen stations in minutes, muttering the prayers at speed, and spend the rest of the time relighting candles that have blown out or clearing the dribbled wax of burned out candles from the holders at the shrine in the church.

Come All Souls' night, my mother and myself set off for the church and cemetery to pray for the speedy release of the souls in Purgatory. Because the main graveyard is a mile outside the village we settle for the murky cemetery in the grounds of St James' Church of Ireland. Getting there on a wild, blackberry night involves crossing the School Lane and then going down Church Lane – both unlit – before squeezing through the stile in the old stone wall. Once inside the wall, the aged, creaking trees close in above and about us, their heavy branches reaching from the dark to tap our shoulders and touch our faces as we make our way between the headstones, trying to locate the path that borders the old church.

There, in the shadow of the stone walls, beneath the barely visible silhouette of the 10th century round tower, we begin our quiet decades of the rosary, my mother leading and me responding with the Our Father, the ten Hail Mary's and the Glory be to the Father. And then we repeat the prayers again and again and again and again until the five decades are done. All the while, we circle the church slowly, picking our way through the darkness, hugging the wall for fear of stumbling over a fallen headstone or cross. Once the five decades of the rosary have been recited, we're into the home straight with just the *Hail Holy Queen* to come. I gallop my way through it: *Hail, holy Queen, Mother of Mercy! Hail our life, our sweetness, and our hope! To thee do we cry, poor banished children of Eve, to thee do we send up our sighs, mourning and weeping in this valley of tears. Turn, then, most gracious advocate, thine eyes of mercy towards us; and after this our exile show unto us the blessed fruit of thy womb Jesus; O clement, O loving, O sweet virgin Mary. Pray for us, O holy Mother of God, that we may be made worthy of the promises of Christ. Amen.*

'Slow down,' my mother says. 'The souls in Purgatory are depending on these prayers for their release.' And then, and not for the first or last time, she adds: 'You'll be glad of someone's prayers if ever you end up there.' And, with that, she goes back to the start and recites the prayer all over again, very, very slowly.

One November night, as we make our rounds of the church, whispering our quiet prayers, a figure looms suddenly out of the darkness. In our concentration on praying and not stumbling we haven't heard the approach of the form which now stands before us, an uncertain shape in the pitch blackness.

'Good evening, Mrs MacKenna,' it says, the strange voice coming from somewhere, just there beyond reach. 'Good evening, John.'

My mother relaxes, breathes out and replies: 'Good evening, Mrs McDonald.'

I feel the sweat begin to pool, then dry on my back. And off they go, immersed in a long and rambling conversation. Normally, I would have wandered away and made my own amusement but, here and now, wandering away would mean playing among the headstones and flat-tabled tombs of the past three hundred years and that is not something I'm prepared to do in the darkness.

In daylight the graveyard is a regular playground, not just for me but for many of the village children. Its twisted stones and fallen crosses, its uneven ground and dips and mounds are the stuff of Hollywood to us ten-year-old gunslingers and Indians. But now, in the deep pitch of a windy November night, it is alien territory. Better by far to stay near the wall and ride out the storm of conversation. And then it's done and we go on our way while Mrs McDonald continues her rounds of the church.

On our way but not quite finished. Crossing the long walkway of the Laurels, we come out on Abbey Street, opposite the parish priest's house, and then we're into the Parish Church and the bizarre experience that will win further free days for the souls in Purgatory by visiting the church, saying an Our Father, Hail Mary and Glory. Each church visit brings an indulgence of a certain number of days to trapped souls but, in order to make the visits count, we have to step outside the church door and then step in again. The whole thing reminds me of a song I've heard my father sing, "Lanigan's Ball." And, my mother assures me; each new visit brings a further indulgence and is a step closer to the release of some poor unfortunate from the misery of Purgatory.

But I grow tired of the cold air outside and busy myself at my preferred task at the shrine in front of the altar, transferring the candles into neat rows, removing the burnt out stumps and relighting flames that have been extinguished by the constant opening and closing of the door as a handful of people come and go. My mission however is interrupted by a sharp pinch on the arm and my mother's voice whispering in my ear: 'Would you, for God's sake, attend to your prayers' and back I traipse to the carousel of opening and closing the creaking door, of cold and a little less coldness, to the prayers that will, I hope, free another soul from the pits of dark sin and punishment.

As November wears on, things at home become more and more tense. The stomach aches, the constant uncertainty that melts into fear once six o'clock strikes without my father being home become more intense. The Friday night and Saturday night drinking become regular rather than occasional and the atmosphere in the house staggers between a deadly silence and ferocious arguments. In desperation, one Sunday night, while my parents are sitting downstairs in silence, I take a Pioneer Abstinence pin from my good jacket and pin it on the lapel of my father's railway uniform jacket. Why? In my eleven-year-old head this is my only way of asking him to change his habits.

The following morning I come downstairs in trepidation but nothing is said. As we sit at the breakfast table, I notice that the pin has been removed from his lapel.

That night, when my mother comes up to turn off my bedroom light, she asks if I'm the one who put the pin on my father's jacket. I nod but she says nothing, just smiles, tucks me in and kisses my forehead.

Something changes in the following weeks. The late night drinking stops and my parents seem happier, easier with each other, determined not to fight. One Sunday night, about two weeks before Christmas, we're in the sitting room, listening to a programme on the radio. I'm playing with my toys on the floor. From the kitchen comes the smell of a Christmas cake baking. The fire is lighting and all seems well with the world. For some reason I glance up from my game and see that my parents are holding hands, seated side by side on the couch. This is something I have never seen before and I sense my small heart soaring.

Later, after my mother has said goodnight, my father comes up and lies on Jarlath's bed and tells me the story of the night he fought the bull on the bridge at Kilkea. It's a story I've heard a hundred times but I lie there and listen to every word with the enthusiasm of someone who has never heard it before. And then my father drifts off to sleep, as he often does, and I close my eyes and, for the first time in weeks, I don't pull the covers over my head to muffle the sound of arguing downstairs.

Later still, I wake and turn to check the time on my bedside clock. It's two in the morning and my father has gone back to my parents' room. I smile and fall asleep again.

Those good times last through the Christmas and into the early weeks of the following year but then life drifts back to how it seems it has always been and, when the football season starts again, I'm sent off on Sundays, my white flag under my arm, accompanying my father to Kildare games.

'What would he want with going to a match? Sure, he'd be bored,' my father will sometimes say.

'He likes football. Don't you?' my mother fires back.

I nod. I do like football. I love the game. I love the excitement. I love the starchy white jerseys of the Kildare team: I love the smells of cut grass and cigarette smoke on the air; I love the way the crowd rises and the noise climbs whenever one of the Kildare players scores; I love the ice-cream sellers wandering up and down the terraces shouting 'Get the last of your Lukey lukeys, last of the choc-ices'; I love the paper hats and the rosettes that are sold outside the grounds; I love when my father lifts me on his shoulders so I can get a better view of the game. What I don't like is the drive home if we stop for 'a bottle of minerals' because then I know we'll be late and my mother will be annoyed and my father will have had a few, which is always a few too many. He's not a heavy drinker but he gets silly when he drinks – repetitive and irritating. Stupid, my mother calls it.

'Why would you be dragging a young fellow into a public house with you?'

'Well, if you hadn't insisted on sending him, I wouldn't be dragging him with me to the match.'

'Oh yes and you'd be falling in here at all hours. Bad and all as this is, it'd be worse.'

'Can a man not have a drink without having to listen to this tirade?'

'A drink! If it was only a drink, I wouldn't mind. But it's never a drink. It's never just one.'

And so the cycle starts again.

Brother Ghost

'"The dead arose and appeared to many."'

I was a late sleeper, especially at Christmas holiday time, and you never missed the chance to quote Matthew 27 at me as I came, heavy-eyed, down the stairs and into the kitchen. And now I wish those words were true, that the dead arose and appeared, that you would appear to me.

I close my eyes and as so often, we're walking the beach at Emerald Isle in North Carolina and we're rattling on about where we'd most like to be and who we'd most like to chat with over dinner.

'Anyone,' you ask, 'living or dead?'

'Anyone,' I say.

And you reel off a handful of names and then I reel off my list and we dissect each other's roll-call. And when that's done we talk about other things, about our lives, about love and loss and hope and we say things that seem important in the late sunshine. We pause and illustrate a point, hands moving in the golden, evening light. In my head, in my imagination, we finish that conversation we began on the beach, without gratuitous politeness, without beating about the bush. We say the things we need to say, once and for all.

If I could redraw that list and have the dead arise and appear at my dinner table, you'd be there at the head of it, smiling, laughing, enjoying every moment of the evening laid out before us. And my happiness would be complete.

Son

I was coming through Dublin's Heuston Station on a wet, miserable Wednesday afternoon when a man sitting on one of the seats near the coffee shops called me. He was a man I knew and we hadn't seen each other in more than a year. The conversation travelled down sidings and then, just before we parted, he said: 'Lal MacKenna was your aunt, wasn't she?'

'She was,' I said.

'I remember her from when I was a boy,' the man said. 'I remember her walking out with …' and he named a man I didn't know. 'They made a lovely couple. I'd see them down the line or on the Square. I could never understand why they didn't stay together. She never married and he never married, either. He was mad about her. What a shame.'

On the train, I thought about my aunt Lal, my father's sister. The quiet woman who was a constant fixture in the kitchen of her sister and brother-in-law's shop; the woman whose life was a continuum of service to others; the woman who raised one family and then another without ever having a child of her own.

Lal was eight when her mother died and she and her three brothers and younger sister were taken into care by their grandmother. A few years later, the children returned to live with their father in Athy. By then, he had remarried and the five children looked forward to a more stable life together, in their new home in the railway cottage on the edge of the town. Within a short time, their step-mother died, leaving Lal to look after her siblings. She was thirteen years old. The year was 1915. She was responsible for cooking and cleaning and running the house. Her teenage years were spent in looking after others, getting them through school and out into the world. She continued to live with and look after her father until his death in 1948.

I thought of the story the man had told me in the station and I wondered whether Lal had been so trapped in the service of others that she had, in some way, become a woman of no great expectations. And I thought of her in her twenties and thirties, walking out with this man who worked in the local foundry. Did she long for children of her own or was she already tired of the notion of motherhood? Was that the reason they never married? If so, there was to be an irony in that fact.

When Lal's father died, she moved in with her sister, Kathleen, and Kathleen's husband, Andy. Andy ran a thriving grocery shop, tea rooms and a boarding house and Lal became carer for Andy and Kathleen's six children; cook for the half-dozen lodgers, and waitress in the tea-rooms. After her sister's death, in 1963, she continued to work and live over the shop until, finally, it was sold. Only then, in the last years of her life, did she find a house and home of her own. She died at the age of seventy-one.

To me, visiting the house where she worked in my childhood and teens, she was my father's older sister, a woman of indeterminate age; sometimes smiling, sometimes bad-tempered. A woman who provided hearty dinners and teas. A woman who offered advice now and then. A woman who worried about her siblings, a woman who never spoke of her own ambitions and dreams.

What I never saw was the woman I'd heard about on the station platform, the young woman who walked out with a young man who loved her. A young woman who might have had another life, a time of her own, in a home of her own, with or without children. Instead she was Lal MacKenna, child-minder, cook, waitress, daughter, sister, shadow. Lal, a woman without even a name of her own, for her given name – one I never heard spoken until the day of her funeral – was Ellen.

Brother Ghost

That extraordinary night when my mother called a halt to the rosary before the trimmings had even begun, something I'd never seen happen before and never would again. It was in the summer of my second year in boarding school and you were home for the weekend. Within seconds, she and our father had disappeared upstairs.

You sat down by the fire. I could sense your unease.

'The mother wants me to talk to you about the facts of life,' you said.

'We did those in school,' I said. 'Norry did them in religion class.'

You breathed a long sigh of relief. You might be studying medicine but this, obviously, was not something you'd signed up for.

'And have you any questions?'

I shrugged and shook my head.

'Right,' you said. 'Well we'd better pretend we're going through the drill. We'll play a couple of games of cards before we head up to bed – that'll keep her happy.'

Father

It was a Saturday afternoon and four of us lads were in Cope's shop, working our way slowly through the departments. We'd sidled in the door of the hardware section, stopping to look at the wooden boxed-shelving that stretched to the ceiling, each box containing nails, screws or fuses of differing sizes. I'd always been amazed at how the shop-assistants in their brown shop coats knew exactly which box to reach for when I handed them the nail or screw or fuse I'd been told to get matched.

Behind us, in the little caboose that served as a cash desk, Miss Harrison was unfolding a docket and taking the money from it; stamping a receipt; parcelling the change into the receipt and replacing it in the metal container that she'd screw back onto a pulley and send flying along the wires that criss-crossed the ceilings of the various departments, the metal cups whizzing by each other but, to our great disappointment, never colliding.

'Tell your mammy I said hello,' she said quietly to me.

'I will, Miss Harrison.'

We moved on, the three of us, aware that loitering breeds suspicion. The trick was to look as though you were going somewhere, as though you were in the shop for a purpose, on a message for your mother, rather than simply passing time, *up to God knows what devilment and no good*, as the manager would quickly tell us.

The grocery department was filled with the smell of fresh bread.

'That'd put the hunger on ya,' one of my companions said, furtively peeling the end from a batch loaf and stuffing it into his mouth. I was relieved that Miss Harrison didn't work in that particular department. That was something she wouldn't miss and something my mother would hear about.

Three of us moved on, the fourth slithered off to see if he could cadge a penny toffee from his aunt who worked behind one of the counters.

'I dare you go to into the drapery section,' one of my companions said.

The response came quick and curt: 'I will in me hole.'

'Cowardy custard.'

'Do you think I'm going in there, where there's women looking at knickers and things? You go in, if you're that mad for it!'

'You have your shite,' the first boy said.

'But you expected me to!'

'Lads, lads, lads, lads!' The toffee chaser came running, almost breathless from the far end of the shop.

'What?'

'Mrs McD is below and she's taking off her clothes, she says she's getting into bed, down below near the bacon counter. Honest to Jesus.'

We followed him quickly, whispering and sniggering but, by the time we reached the lower end of the shop, three women had surrounded Mrs McD and were helping her on with her coat and hat.

'Away with ye!' one of them ordered and we knew by her tone that she wasn't joking.

Later that evening, as we sat at the tea table, the coded conversation began.

'There was a bit of an event with Mrs McD in Cope's today,' my mother said.

'Is that so? What happened?' my father asked, the question terse, not giving anything away.

'Miss Harrison told me. Mrs McD thought she was at home. Was getting ready to go to bed.'

'That's not a good sign.'

'No.'

'It's a good thing that you didn't make a fuss when she got that order mixed up at Christmas.'

'Indeed it is. I'd be mortified if I had.'

A silence eased into the conversation and then my father spoke, his voice low and mysteriously serious.

'It might be an idea to go down and talk to Frank, in case he doesn't know the lie of the land.'

'I think you're right. I think it'd be a holy and a wholesome thought. I'll go down after I do the washing up.'

'I'll look after the washing up,' my father said. 'I think the quicker you go down the more help it might be.'

'Isn't it a sad situation?' my mother said as she put on her coat.

'It is. We never know when we're well off.'

Brother Ghost

I received a letter from Canada, from Jim Byrne, your classmate in Castledermot. A few weeks later, we spoke on the phone and he told me stories of you that I had never heard. He talked about his first day at school and how the gates of the schoolyard had seemed like prison bars until our mother came, smiling, to meet him.

He talked about how you'd become best buddies; about the wooden garden gate of our house on the Low Terrace; about playing cowboys with you – Hopalong Cassidy and Roy Rogers; about the luxury of jam and bread in the back garden; about your black cowboy hat; about the rabbits you kept in a hutch; about your version of the Grand National, run over fences in Whelan's garden.

And he told a story of you both being allowed to go and play in the old Franciscan Abbey, on the understanding that you would not climb the crumbling walls in search of jackdaws' nests. So, instead, you both clambered to the top of the east window and sat there, dangerously high in the air, catapulting stones at a turnip in the disused baptism font below.

As I listened, you were alive again. You were the young boy I never knew. I had a treasured glimpse into the first ten years of your life and I laughed with you and Jim, galloped with you and watched as you rode the swing in our yard like a covered wagon. But I stayed safely on the ground while the pair of you scaled the treacherous heights of the Abbey window.

Father

A Friday afternoon in the late autumn, and, as ever, my mother was rushing to finish a letter. Always, late in the afternoon, she seemed to be finishing some letter, her neat handwriting spreading out across the pages as she sat at the kitchen table.

'Don't you go too far away,' she said. 'I'll want you in a minute to run up with this to the Post Office.'

There always seemed to be an urgency in the writing and posting of these epistles. But then that was hardly surprising. She'd finish teaching at 3 o'clock and by the time the tidying up was done and the school building checked and locked it could be well after half past three. And then there was the daily trip to the church to make the Stations of the Cross and there might or might not be people to talk to on the road home. Usually there were, conversations that left me kicking stones and sighing.

'Just one more note to write,' my mother called. I came and stood beside her at the kitchen table. Her pen racing from line to line, beautiful handwriting that spilled elegantly over the paper. I looked through the sealed envelopes of the letters already written. Addresses in Dublin and Tuam and Birmingham. Friends and relatives, one of the Kinsellas – they were our neighbours on the Low Terrace; they practically raised me for the first four years of my life until, one by one, the girls emigrated to Birmingham. Nan, my favourite, was the last to go.

'Right,' my mother said, 'that's the last one.' She sealed the envelope and handed me the stamp money. 'Now, run like the wind.' And off I shot, stopping briefly to open the front gate. It was a ritual of mine. I'd open the gates so that when my father got home from work he could drive straight in. It was a ritual and an act of faith. Then my father would go through his ritual of closing the gates once the car was inside.

That done, I was away – running through the other rituals. Naming the names of the families who lived in the houses I passed: O'Connells; Mulhalls; McGlades; Healys; Jenkinsons; Kanes; Dowlings; Devereills; Byrnes. Then Mat Neill's house; Kinsella's; Paddy Byrne's; O'Flaherty's; Hennesy's; the Cobbler Lawler's and up through the village; over the Square, past Gannon's Pub; The Shamrock Bar; Hennessy's garage and across the empty road to the Post Office.

Inside, Carrie Murphy was emptying the post box.

'The nick of time,' she said, taking the money while I stamped the envelopes.

The return journey was less frantic. I sauntered back along the street, stopping to look in Cope's window at the soundless television, telling its black and white stories of adventure. On the corner, the silent men dragged life and light from their Woodbine butts. And then I was on the road home, back the way I'd come. Down Abbey Street, past Carlow Gate, up the hill and into Abbeylands. Once I'd breasted the hill I could feel the tightness in my stomach, the knot hardening like a ball of vomit in the hollow of my belly. The act of faith returned. Another ritual took the place of the opening of the gate. I slowed my pace and made deals, promises to God and myself. If a car passed me in the next hundred yards the gates would be closed, my father would be home, all would be well and we'd have our evening meal in peace. If a car didn't pass then the gate would still be open and my father wouldn't be home and if he wasn't home by then, the angelus bell ringing out across the fields, he wouldn't be home for hours. Friday was pay day. If he was home, I'd be good for the rest of the week, I'd keep my thoughts pure and clean.

I slowed my pace, no lights behind, no lights in front, not a sign of a car in either direction. I passed Healy's house; McGlade's; Mulhall's; the spare garden; O'Connell's. The gates were still wide open. My father wasn't home. The knot in my stomach loosened but only momentarily and a sick feeling of disappointment and trepidation rose through my chest and into my throat. I thought I might throw up, but then the nausea subsided, twisting itself again into the small, black glob of fear.

I knew the drill. If my father wasn't home by six, it could be eight or ten or twelve or later. The inevitable row would follow and the rancour would spill through Saturday and Sunday. The weekend would be one of silence, broken by sporadic criticisms between my parents. The well-worn phrases would surface as they always did: *Money to burn. Stop this constant bloody nagging. Not the man I married. I have neither peace nor ease. Could have done so much better. Be better off getting a job in England. Well, don't let me be the one to stop you. Always the bitter word. The worse for wear.* Round and round they'd go while I'd try, from time to time, to make the peace. This, I felt, was my responsibility, this was my duty – to bring the bickering to an end, to restore some kind of harmony, to make them see eye to eye. And sometime the following afternoon I'd take the dogs out for a walk and hope to return to a quiet house, the beginning of a thaw, but, instead, I already knew I'd be greeted by a razor of silence or the sound of voices raised so loud that I'd hear them from halfway down the garden and I'd shrink from everything that lay ahead – the words that would fly like sharpened axes, the silences that would lurk at the back of every chair; the time spent sitting on the stairs, afraid to sleep, afraid to intervene. It seemed to me that I lived in a war-zone that passed for life.

'Friday night is music night,' my mother said. She was ironing and the radio up on the high shelf – beside the picture of the Sacred Heart, with its blessing for the family – was broadcasting BBC Radio 2 and the programme that began in the year I was born. *Friday Night is Music Night* was a regular in our house – like *The Archers* and *Mrs Dale's Diary*. But it had grown to mean something else in the shorthand of familial language. Whenever my father hadn't come straight home from work on Fridays, the programme title took on an irony for my mother and became a signal of danger for me.

A long night lay ahead: bed at half past ten and then a wait for the car lights to turn in through our gateway; the sound of the key in the front door lock; the noise from downstairs and the stumble of my father's boots on the stair. Then, stupidly, the turning on of the light in my parents' bedroom and the slurring of some story about trains running late or thick fog on the road between work and home and the battle would begin, the loud words, the angry voices, the unspoken and spoken resignation and disappointment seeping through the wall from their room into mine before it permeated the whole house and submerged it in the dim light of disenchantment and dread.

Son

Late July 1968, from an open window the sound of Des O'Connor singing "I Pretend" is oozing along the gardens of Abbeylands. I'm cycling back from some escapade out the Mill Road, some search for adventure that has, inevitably, had to be satisfied by the promise of tomorrow.

On the wall between our garden and next door's garden, two women are sitting, chatting in the still-warm sunshine of that summer twilight. One is a tall woman, the other is shorter. The first is our neighbour, Mrs O'Connell, the second is my mother.

Our garden is mostly lawn, with flower beds around the perimeter. O'Connell's garden is filled with hundreds of different varieties of flowers. My mother is an occasional gardener, Mrs O'Connell is, to use her own word, an *avid* gardener. Both women are smoking. Mrs O'Connell draws slowly and deeply on her cigarette with all the ease and practice of a lifetime. My mother puffs and exhales with the unease of a recent convert. As with their gardening, one is an avid smoker, the other is an occasional accomplice.

This moment is frozen in my memory because it comes from a time – ten years after we first moved to 1061 Abbeylands – when my mother and Mrs O'Connell have reached an agreement. For a decade they have referred to each other, through the most intimate and harrowing of times and conversations, as Mrs O'Connell and Mrs MacKenna. But, in recent weeks, there have been overtures; I'm not sure from which side, to move on from the formality of Mrs to the warmer informality of first names.

Mrs O Connell is Brigid but her husband calls her Bride. My mother's given name is Winifred but she has always been Una.

And so, these two women have agreed to break a habit and liberate themselves from being the wives of men called O'Connell and MacKenna and become their own women. The times, indeed, are a changing.

I dismount from my bike outside Kelly's gate, four doors down, and pretend to fiddle with the chain. But I'm watching the two women, sitting side by side on the low wall and I'm taking in the moment. I don't yet know why, but I sense, even as a fifteen-year-old, that this image of recreation and comfort and ease will become important to me at some point in the future.

I know that Tom O Connell is down the river, fishing. He, too, is an avid gardener but fishing is his passion. And I know my father is in our back garden, earthing the potatoes.

Perhaps the moment has an added significance because, earlier in the day, my parents and Mr and Mrs O'Connell drove the mile or so out of Castledermot to Coltstown cemetery to choose their final resting places, plots that lie side by side. Whether the urge to choose the grave sites came from the urge to use first names or whether the use of Christian names came from the talk of final resting places, I'm not sure, but one has been done and paid for and the other is under way.

I stand and watch surreptitiously, see the small scribbles of cigarette smoke write briefly on the still, summer air; hear the fading lines of music from that open window; watch two women lost in a conversation that is theirs and theirs alone. And then I cycle the twenty yards to our house, swing in through the open gateway, the sound of the bicycle tyres on the gravel draws the attention of the two women from the other side of the lawn. They wave and I wave back.

The agreement on Christian names lasts a few weeks but neither woman is comfortable with the arrangement and, by summer's end, they're back to the more familiar, more comfortable Mrs O'Connell and Mrs MacKenna.

And here I am again, on a summery evening, standing now in Coltstown cemetery, reading the headstones on the adjacent plots – Brigid Mary O'Connell and Una MacKenna – reliving that moment from more than half a century ago and picturing the pair of them on the low, garden wall – antirrhinum, aster, nasturtium, wallflower, rose and honeysuckle growing all around them, already drawing them slowly back into the earth from which we all come and to which we all must, in time, return.

Brother Ghost

I envied you so many things. Your maturity, your good looks, your confidence, how you made your way with self-assurance through the world. The one thing I didn't envy you was telling our parents that you didn't want to be a teacher. You'd done your degree in English and History; you'd taken your Higher Diploma in Education. You were qualified as a teacher, four years of college behind you. You were following in our mother's and several of her brothers' and one of her sister's footsteps. This was the early nineteen sixties when a permanent and pensionable job was everything anyone could wish for. Not only that, but you'd got a job in the local Vocational School. And then you told them you didn't want to be a teacher; you wanted to study medicine.

I don't remember that day, that conversation, but I do know they thought it a fad, something that had grown out of the fact that we had cousins who were studying medicine and veterinary medicine. But you persuaded them – on one condition: that you'd go straight through, no repeat years. You passed your exams or you were out – that was the deal. That and working in England in the summers to help towards the fees. It was a huge undertaking on your part and on theirs. Finances were tight – were they ever any other way?

And now I look at those old photographs of you and the other young men I got to know when they came and stayed or passed through the house on autumn or Christmas afternoons. Students like yourself – Des Sleator and John Conway and Malachy Darcy and Ted Rowlette. The names were like magic potions to my ears. They were your friends and they seemed so nonchalant and calm and classy and they appeared to know what the world was about and where they were bound within it. And I was the child who was terrified of the night and the harsh words it might, and often did, bring through the floorboards from the kitchen below. I wanted so much to be you, to be away, to be self-assured. I wanted to know my place in the world rather than running from it.

When I think of Christmases back then, I think of you. You brought peace on earth and goodwill into my life. I stopped worrying about our parents' squabbles when you were in the house. You were the one who brought home that first record player. You were the one who borrowed LPs from Frank McDonald. You were the one who entertained us for hours with that reel to reel tape recorder, impersonating the local characters, catching their idiosyncrasies, bringing them alive to my ears. You were the one who sang that bizarre version of "O Holy Night" in the voice of a drunken singer on his way home from the pub, changing the lyrics and miming the *fall on your knees* line as he collapsed outside his hall door. You were the one who drank half the Christmas cream and replaced it with milk and then stood by, your face the picture of innocence, as I tried and tried unsuccessfully, perspiration running down my face, to whisk and thicken it. You were the one who went to parties in Carlow and regaled us with stories that made me envy your grown-up life.

Let me tell you a story, brother. It's a story I wanted to tell you when we walked the beach in Virginia but I never found a way into it, I think because it frightened me and frightens me still.

It was a night in spring, just before or after Easter. There was no rain, no frost, my memory is that the night outside was mild and calm. I was wakened sometime around midnight by the arguing downstairs. Now that I'm older and have been through the harsh words and door-slamming myself, I know things aren't always as bad as they sound to the child on the stairs. But when you're ten years old and your world is a carousel of the highs of just living on the edge, followed by the lows of nights that make the world a verbal scrapyard, the words, the sounds, the tones become the things you learn to read for the shade and hint that tells you how long the argument will go on and how fierce it will become and what the after-effects may be.

On that spring night, the words came scorching and intense and the banging of the back door told me this was more serious than most of the arguments I'd heard. I didn't wait. I pulled on my trousers and shirt and jumper, wriggled my feet into my sandals and went down the stairs, my hands pressed hard against each wall, taking four steps at a time. I was gone, through the front door, before our father had time to see or hear me.

Once outside, I scanned the road but there was no one to be seen in the faint light from the streetlamps. Something told me – intuition, instinct or terror – to go in the opposite direction, down the garden path, out over the fence that separated our vegetable garden from the football field. Once out there, beyond the fence, I ran and ran towards the river. And that's where I found our mother, at the gate that separated the football field from Keatley's field and the low, slow river beyond. That gate topped off with rolls of barbed wire.

'I thought you were gone,' I said.

'I was going,' she said. 'I can't go back. I can't put up with this drinking night after night.'

I don't know how long we stood at the gate of that field, she in her dress and me my short-trousers and sandals while the moon and stars dragged themselves across the sky, but it seemed to me that the woman and the small boy who stood there with his mother, at the razored gate beside the little field with the low river beyond it, were the most forlorn people in the loneliest place in the world and nothing would ever make any of this right again.

Eventually, I persuaded her to come back home with me. We trudged across the football field and I held the wire fence while she slipped through it and we walked up the garden.

The back door was unlocked and we went inside. The fire was dead but the kitchen was still warm. I know it was a Friday night because we didn't have to be up for school the next morning. I made tea and we sat and talked about my father; about drinking; about what might and might not happen; about getting away, starting anew somewhere else; about all those things that would never happen. And then we went to bed. And early the following morning I heard our father slip downstairs and leave for work – he never missed a day. And the following night he was late home again, late and stupidly drunk. But that night there was no running away, just the callous words and the raised voices and the knowledge that the next day would be a silence broken by intermittent arguments.

I still don't know for sure why our father drank. Perhaps he was deeply unhappy. Perhaps he felt life hadn't been good to him. Perhaps he was drowning childhood memories like the memories I'm sharing with you now. But back then I had no notion about any of that. All I had were the experiences of waking in the night and leaving with, or searching for, our mother when she couldn't take any more.

And, yes, there were other nights like that – our mother walking through the fields; leaving home with a suitcase and doing three rounds of the Green before going back home; wishing, wishing, wishing that you were there because you could make life better, could make this madness go away, could mend this sadness that seeped into every pore of my life in those days and nights when the world seemed full of bitterness and unhappiness and dread. Most of all, dread.

Father

A summer night in the August of 1968. I'd completed my Inter Cert exams at St Clement's College in Limerick and I was picking up odds and ends of work from neighbours. Grass-cutting and block-chopping in the main, bits of weeding and watering of gardens while people were away on holiday.

There was a carnival and a marquee on The Green. I went down to the carnival most nights with its chair-o-planes, bumpers, swinging-boats, its pongo tent and rifle range. I wandered around the place with Pat Clowry or Michael Finn or on my own, mostly laughing and chatting; sometimes taking a spin on the bumpers; always on the lookout for girls, who never seemed to be on the lookout for us.

On Friday and Saturday and Sunday nights there were dances in the marquee but I didn't ask if I could go, not because I'd be refused permission by my mother (which I would) but because, if by some miracle she said *yes*, I'd be astray in a world I couldn't handle and didn't understand. The youth club hops were fine, though more often than not I ended up in the room where discussions and arguments about changing the world were going on, rather than in the room where the music was playing and people were dancing. I spent more time analysing the lyrics of "MacArthur Park" than I did dancing to "Mony Mony" or "Congratulations."

On that summer Sunday night, I was lying in bed reading. It was well after midnight and the windows in the lads' room – my room for now, my brother was away working for the summer – were thrown wide into the still and summery air outside. The tinny music from the carnival had ended, to be replaced by the sounds of the warm-up band in the marquee. And then, sometime into that early hour, I heard the rough and ragged tones of Ronnie Drew and the Dubliners travelling across the darkness and I was suddenly wide awake.

The previous summer the Dubliners had had a huge hit with "Seven Drunken Nights," a song that intrigued me, more for its being banned on RTE Radio than for any inherent depth in its lyric. Any version I'd ever heard played on other radio stations stopped at verse five.

And as I went home on Friday night as drunk as drunk could be
I saw a head upon the bed where my old head should be
Well, I called me wife and I said to her: Will you kindly tell to me
who owns that head upon the bed where my old head should be?
Ah, you're drunk,
you're drunk, you silly old fool,
still you cannot see
that's a baby boy that me mother sent to me
Well, it's many a day I've travelled a hundred miles or more
but a baby boy with his whiskers on sure I never saw before

If the band was playing live, which it was; and if the people wanted to hear "Seven Drunken Nights," which they did, then this was my chance to catch the missing, exciting, sexually-charged closing verses. I jumped out of bed and pushed the windows open even wider, leaning out to check that I could hear the lyrics clearly. At that moment they were singing the "Black Velvet Band." I got back into bed and went on reading, one ear on the music drifting up from the village.

Twenty minutes passed and then I caught the opening chords and I was up like a shot, leaning as far out the window as I could to hear every word. And, sure enough, the lyrics came crystal clear through the balmy night – the Monday verse about the horse; the Tuesday verse with the coat behind the door; the Wednesday verse with the pipe upon the chair; the Thursday verse with the boots that pass for geranium pots and into the Friday verse with the head upon the bed. And then a voice rose, Lazarus-like, from the lawn below.

'Are you all right up there?'

I looked down to see my father looking up at me. He was on his way out to close the front gates.

'Just listening to the music,' I said.

'What verse are they on?'

'Friday.'

'Well, you'll be disappointed,' he said quietly. 'You don't think they'll sing Saturday and Sunday with the P.P. in the marquee?'

'How do you know he's in the marquee?'

'He's always there – if not in body then in spirit, as the fellow says.' And with that the song came to an end, the bellowing of the crowd – disappointed or frustrated – rising above the closing notes, the whistling and cheering swelling into the darkness above us.

'What did I tell you?' my father said. 'Body or spirit,' and he crossed the lawn, chuckling to himself while the Dubliners launched into "Maids When You're Young Never Wed an Old Man" and I went back to my book.

Brother Ghost

You used to laugh at me if I went on a twenty-mile cycle. 'Mother Ireland, you're rearing them yet,' you'd say. I had you down for someone who had never been interested in pushing yourself beyond the bounds of staying fit and keeping healthy. Yes, you'd played basketball for the school and, yes, you played football with me when you were home from college.

At that stage I was borrowing Mrs O'Connell-next-door's bike to get me to and from my summer job as assistant gardener to Father Eoin in the Cistercian monastery at Bolton Abbey. I had visions of a sparkling new bike. It would be black. Or red. One speed but sleek and fast. It wouldn't have the bulky basket that Mrs O'Connell's bike had, the woven intricacy which caught the wind, even speeding down Bolton Hill, and lifted the front of the bike like an overloaded plane trying ineffectively to leave the ground. A basket that once lifted me into the path of a passing truck and sent me flying into the ditch, landing on my back, relieved to have survived and even more relieved that Mrs O'Connell's bike was undamaged.

When I went cycling with my friends we'd be strung out over half a mile, the fellows with the stripped down, rebuilt, no mudguards/no baskets/no carriers models way out in front; the fellows with normal bicycles somewhere in the middle and fellows like me on High-Nellies bringing up the rear.

And now, with the ball spinning up and down the lawn, in a race to twenty goals and a fifteen seven lead under my belt, I'm feeling confident. I can almost smell the new scent of the leather saddle and the invitation of the spotless, rubber tyres. I can almost hear the ring of the tightened bell and feel the grasp of the handlebars as my fists close over them. No more slogging behind, no more arriving home to find the rest of the gang has long dispersed, no more dismounting to push up hills like Sisyphus. Everything will change when I become the owner of this shining promise. Make that sixteen-seven!

You call a halt.

'Time for a glass of lemonade.'

We sit on the step outside the back-kitchen, the sun on our faces.

'When are you going back to Dublin?' I ask.

'Probably on Friday.'

I nod but my heart sinks. I'd hoped you'd be here for the weekend. But I kind of understand. If I could get away, I think I would, too.

'Right, time to get stuck in,' you say, downing the last of your lemonade and patting my head. Is that because you want to encourage me or it because you know what your leaving means to me? Dolores is away teaching so I'll be an only child again, once you've gone back to Dublin. Just as you once were.

Father

We had a potato pit at the foot of the garden, the year's crop covered with clay and straw to protect it from the winter frosts and snow, enough potatoes to see us through until the spring. I never minded being sent to pick Brussels sprouts in the depths of winter, there was a satisfaction in twisting the hard green globes from the frozen stalks. Being sent to get potatoes from the pit was another thing entirely.

The pit occasionally drew rats, particularly in the hard, frozen days of January and February. They'd come nosing from the ditches in search of food. The trick was to always check for signs of their burrowing before opening the pit. But, sometimes, it was late in the afternoon when I was despatched, basin and torch in one hand, spade in the other, to bring in the potatoes for that day's dinner. I'd listen for rustling, imagining I heard the slithery scrabbling of rodents at every turn of the clay. Grabbing a handful of potatoes and then another, whistling or singing all the while, to keep the animals at bay, I'd be there and gone as quickly as I could.

There was an evening in early summer. My mother came back, ashen-faced, from the shed.

'What's wrong?' I asked.

'There's a rat in the shed.'

'Are you sure it's not a mouse?'

'It's a rat.'

I wanted to have the courage to go out and deal with it, take this one problem off her plate but I was terrified.

Later, my father arrived home from work. My mother was in the kitchen, preparing the evening meal.

'We have a visitor in the shed,' she said. 'A big one!'

'Right,' my father said quietly. 'I'll deal with it.'

'Do you want to leave it till after your tea?'

'Not at all. I'll have it done by the time the tea is wet.'

I watched him step outside and pull his socks up over the ends of his trousers; rats had a reputation for running up trouser legs when cornered. He took a spade from where it was leaning against the wall of the house, shot the bolt on the shed door and stepped inside, closing the door behind him.

I went out into the yard and stood in the birdsong, listening. No great noise, just boxes being moved quietly from one side of the shed to the other, a short scuffle of feet turning and then the sound of the same boxes being returned to their proper locations. *A place for everything and everything in its place*, my father would say.

Finally, the shed door opened and my father stepped out, the corpse of a large rat dangling over the edges of the spade.

'His running days are over,' my father said and smiled.

I watched him walk the length of the garden and deposit the dead rat on a bonfire he was preparing. And then he came back up and leaned the spade against the shed wall.

'I wish I could do that,' I said.

'Why would you?' my father asked. 'Sure amn't I here to do it?'

And then we went inside, he washed his hands and we sat to begin our evening meal.

Brother Ghost

One of the things I missed when you left for America, what I missed every time you went away to work or went back to boarding school or college was our life in *the lads' room*. The laughter we had together. The pranks we got up to – or more often the practical jokes you put me up to. Tying string to Dolores' bedroom window next door and slowly, creakingly opening it while she was reading in bed, terrifying her and bringing our father storming into our room, where he found me still hanging out the window, laughing, while you feigned sleep in the other bed.

And the days after you came back from summer work in England. The questions I had for you and the tales – tall and otherwise – you told about your adventures in London. The ghost-stories that scared the living daylights out of me: the ghost of a British soldier sitting on your bed in the flat on Leeson Street; the ghost air-hostess you picked up hitching near Shannon airport, her hair and clothes bone-dry in the middle of a stormy downpour.

And the short trips home between returning from America and going back to college. That cassette of Jeannie C. Riley and "Harper Valley PTA" and "Widow Jones and Mr Harper" and "Run Jeannie Run." Strong stuff for our house in 1968. I played that cassette so often that it snagged in the cassette player and I spent an hour locked in the bathroom, cassette, scissors, nail file and sticky tape to hand, trying to get the whole thing back together again and running smoothly.

The other music you brought home was an LP called *The Blue and the Grey*, songs of the American Civil War. I was enthralled. This was music I'd never heard or even heard of at the time.

And when you left, all that was gone. The lads' room became my room. The albums and cassettes that I played were the ones I bought. Things reverted to black and white.

Son

There's something about the taste of toothpaste and the smell of floor polish that remind me of boarding school. The floor polish smell is obvious. Every time we walked through the front door of St Clement's college after holidays the smell that met us was of freshly waxed floors. The tiles gleamed in the September afternoons and whatever light was in the sky caught the sparkle and danced it before us.

But now it's the taste of the toothpaste, the sharp, minty taste in my throat that takes me back to the dormitory in Limerick and the sounds of laughter and the silence that fell the moment the doors swung open and the priest on duty began his nightly rounds.

Once I'd settled in, I loved boarding school. I enjoyed the fun; the plays and the debating and the fraternity of the boys who were my fellow students. In theory, we were all potential priests and the school was intended to take us in that direction but, in fact, what we got was a full and rounded, liberal education. Perhaps that was because I arrived in the wake of Vatican II when doors were opening and new ideas were part of our daily lives.

Not that my first three months at St Clement's were a joy. I was desperately lonely. Jarlath, who had left five years before my arrival, was well remembered for his academic prowess and for his stage presence. He'd been the Pirate King in *The Pirates of Penzance* in his final year.

I remembered him singing about the house when I was a small boy:

Oh better far to live and die

under the brave black flag I fly
than play a sanctimonious part
with a pirate head and a pirate heart.
Away to the cheating world go you,
where pirates all are well to do,
but I'll be true to the song I sing
and live and die a Pirate king.

And I remember the hours it took my father to drive to Limerick in the Morris Minor to see and hear my brother on stage. He looked ten feet tall in his pirate outfit, a huge feathered hat on his head, a sword in his hand. I was as proud as punch and I think that was the night I began to believe that nothing bad would ever happen to me as long as he was around.

By the time I arrived at St Clement's, Jarlath was making his way through medical school. By the time I was in Leaving Cert he was married and practising in America. But, in those first few months of homesickness, as I wondered whether I could ever survive; as I worried about the state of my parents' marriage; as our French teacher reminded us daily that *the first seven years are the worst, gentlemen*, my brother's shadow fell heavily on my shoulders.

By the time I'd reached fifth year, I walked with my own shadow behind me – walked and ran and played football and basketball but, like my sixteen class comrades, I had never learned to dance. And that is where Miss Sylvia Leigh-Doyle stepped into my life. To our amazement – this being an all-boys, all-boarders, Redemptorist Juniorate with less than a hundred pupils and just one female teacher – our then headmaster informed us that we would be having dancing classes with Miss Leigh-Doyle and we were to behave ourselves like the gentlemen he was endeavouring to make of us! Which we did – fear, indeed terror, of anyone of the opposite sex being a great regulator. And when this young, slim, athletic woman appeared in the common room we were in awe of her. Collectively and instantly, the seventeen of us fell in love with her. And in that magic number – seventeen – lay the fulfilment of our dreams. Seventeen boys learning to waltz, each with a male partner from the class, left an odd-man-out every week and that odd-man-out got to dance with Miss Leigh-Doyle.

My turn came and my turn went, my heart pounding in my chest, my eyes on the floor, trying to keep control of my two left feet. We twirled, she and I, to Engelbert Humperdinck's "The Last Waltz." That was another great thing about Sylvia Leigh-Doyle, she didn't bring in Strauss records for our dancing lessons, she brought in music we knew and loved. And among the bundle of singles and albums she deposited beside the radiogram was *Parsley, Sage, Rosemary and Thyme*. Sometimes, when our dancing came to an early halt, she'd let us listen to records in the common room. I was enthralled by several of the tracks on the Simon and Garfunkel album but particularly "For Emily, Whenever I May Find Her."

On our last day before the Easter holidays I was listening to the album, gently replacing the stylus for the fifth time at the start of track 4 on side 2 when a voice at my shoulder said: 'You seem to like that song.'

'I like the whole album,' I stammered.

'Well, why don't you take it home with you for the Easter holidays?'

'Are you serious?'

'Absolutely. Take it with you.'

Despite her best efforts, I didn't learn to dance, but I learned to revere the songs of Paul Simon and I got to borrow Sylvia Leigh-Doyle's album for ten days, and I went on being in love with its owner for the rest of that year.

Brother Ghost

I have very little memory of your wedding. I don't even remember for sure what I wore – I think it was a morning suit but I'm not certain. There are photographs of Clare and you together and photographs of Clare and you with our parents but I've never found one in which I appear. I don't even remember if there was an official photographer at the wedding – probably not. It was in University Church on Stephen's Green but the rest is a blur.

I do remember having a wild idea that I might sing at the reception, as an unexpected surprise, my present to the pair of you. I was sixteen, without so much as a tune in my head, and I got this notion that I could sing "My Cup Runneth Over." I'd been listening to it on a John MacNally LP. MacNally was a past pupil of St Clement's and our French teacher – he of *the first seven years are the worst* remark – had harrumphed when he saw the album cover: a picture of the singer superimposed on a photograph of a beautiful young woman on a beach.

'Well, he wasn't like that when I knew him,' he'd snapped, handing the album back to me and walking away.

I'd learned the lyrics and I practised the song whenever I could, walking around the grounds of the boarding school. But I didn't sing it at the wedding.

I had no voice. I lost my nerve. The opportunity never arose. On the day, I realised that what sounded reasonable in the open air would be a discordant embarrassment in the confines of a hotel dining room.

A few days after the wedding, you and Clare called to the school and we sat in the parlour and talked. You brought me sweets and biscuits. And then you were gone, off to America to start a new life there as a doctor. I thought that the saddest day between us. If only I'd known.

Son

A Friday night, music night. We're sitting at the kitchen table, my mother and I, listening to The Archers.

'What's on in the pictures tonight?' my mother asks.

I tell her.

'And would you like to go?'

I shake my head.

'Why not?'

'Ah, I just wouldn't. I'd say it's not a great film.'

I want to say, 'Why don't the two of us go?' But I know there's no point. She wouldn't come with me and, anyway, if she did, I'd feel odd sitting in what passed for the balcony in the Castle Cinema while my friends sat in the cheap seats down near the front.

'You might enjoy it,' she says.

I want to explain that I wouldn't enjoy it; that my mind would be on whether my father had arrived home; that I'd be wondering what the atmosphere would be when I got back. Or, worse still, I'd trudge up the street and see, again, that the gates were still open, the car was not in the garage, the battle still lay ahead.

'Maybe next week,' I say.

I have no idea what I expected my presence to do for my mother but I do know I felt the need, the responsibility, to *be* there as a verification that she was not alone. I'd be a confidante who would listen. I was twelve years old. In many ways, I still am.

Father

We were the children of the village schoolteacher and that fact brought its own expectations. There were the expectations of our mother, the expectations of the neighbours, the expectations of our fellow pupils in the school and, probably worst of all, the expectations we had of ourselves – the pressures to be hard-working, well-behaved, and *a credit to your mother*. Our lives, it seemed, were to be a series of hyphenated and italicised anticipations, leaving little or no room for us to be ourselves. We were stamped and distinct from the moment of birth. And, in the midst of all this, nobody seemed to remember that we were also the children of our father. We were the railwayman's children, too.

He loved his work and he loved the permanent way and he loved the rolling stock. The names tripping off his tongue were poetry to me: flat-beds; cement wagons; cattle wagons; convertible wagons; Bauxites; hoppers; open wagons; H vans; guards' vans – how, I wondered, could he possibly remember them all.

And he loved the signal cabin and I marvelled at his strength in pulling the signal levers and I sat in awe as he rattled off information to the signalman in Kildare station about the trains that had just left. Just as I marvelled at his strength in shunting wagons, offloading three or four in the siding and coupling another three or four for the onward journey to Waterford. And I revelled in the days when I was allowed to travel on the guard's van from Athy station to the asbestos factory. On summer days, I would stand on the open platform at the back, watching for Jesse James and his gang, and on winter days I'd sit inside, heated by the pot-bellied stove in the middle of the floor, imagining how wonderful it would be to live there, to make this van my home, deciding where I'd sleep and where I'd sit and how I could travel the country and always be that important thing – a railway guard. But that was me – for my father, Athy station was the place he loved and wanted to be.

And he loved the men with whom he laboured, men like Mick Murphy, the signalman. He was proud of his job, of his position as foreman. And he was proud of the idea that he was not just a railway man himself but one in a line of men who worked first for the South-Eastern Railway and, later, for CIE.

If I close my eyes, I see him standing on the top step of the signal cabin stairs, pencil in one hand, penknife in the other, the shavings of pencil wood flying through the air as he sharpens the lead before returning to his high desk inside the door and filling in the numbers of wagons and trucks below. And if I open the drawer of my desk, I'll find that penknife inside.

Son

My parents loved me, of that I have no doubt. And I loved them. My love for them has changed over the years since their deaths. It hasn't diminished but it has altered as I have recognised, more and more, my own faults and weaknesses and come to understand some of the reasons behind their actions and inactions.

What hasn't changed is my questioning of the nature of my parents' relationships with each other. What was it that brought them together and what was it that made them decide they might have a happy and fulfilling life as husband and wife? And when did that happiness begin to lose its sheen – and why? When did those flashes of recognition arrive, those moments when the people to whom they were married no longer seemed to be the people with whom they had fallen in love? And was it simply the mores of the time, and financial demands that kept them together?

Brother Ghost

I assumed, perhaps we all did, that when you moved to the States you'd settle in one place and get on with your life there. But it wasn't to be so. You moved and moved again and again. Always in search of something else, somewhere more suited to your ideas on what a doctor should be and what he should do.

On one visit we found you in Buffalo. It was late April and we drove down from Sabbathday Lake in Maine to visit. And then, on 1 May, it snowed and snowed. We spent an hour knocking the newly fallen snow off the tree branches around the house to save them from breaking under the weight. Back inside, you came up with the idea of having a Christmas dinner to celebrate the snowfall. So we gathered around the table, laden with good food, and you put on some LPs of Christmas carols – 'Never mind that it's the first day of summer,' you said – and we celebrated Christmas together, something we hadn't done in a long, long time.

Finally, years later, you ended up in Duke University in North Carolina and it became a kind of spiritual home for you. And when we visited, you brought us to watch the Duke basketball team, the Blue Devils. You were as passionate about them as I was about Kildare's footballers. You introduced us to Coach K, Mike Krzyzewski. He was your hero.

And when you took early retirement from medicine you told me you were *tired of delivering babies for fourteen-year-old girls* and photography became your passion. I have this postcard you sent us in June 2003, from Kingston in North Carolina. It came in the days after Clare's birthday party.

Hi All, The party was a great success – Tipp jersey was modelled. Photos to follow by email when developed. Presume you have heard of Conrad Aiken, the J Mercer is Johnny of 'Moon River' etc fame. I gave a copy of 'Garden of Good and Evil' to Dolores – borrow it and read it before you come – we can hit Savannah some weekend and Charleston. Think you would enjoy. The brother & old lady.

The card had a photograph of Bonaventure Cemetery in Savannah, the burial place of Mercer and Aiken, the same Aiken who wrote *Separate we come and separate we go, And this be it known, is all that we know*. We were due to visit you the following summer but between one thing and another the visit got postponed to the summer of 2005 and, by then, you were too ill to take us anywhere.

Son

It's July 1973 and the radio is playing in my bedsit in Sandymount in Dublin. Outside, the night sky is still holding light, the tide is far out on the strand and the songs come one after the other – Peters and Lee singing "Welcome Home"; David Bowie with "Life on Mars"; Clifford T. Ward singing "Gaye"; and Paul Simon's "Take Me to the Mardi Gras."

I'm sitting at the little table, the window open onto the night, and I'm writing a letter to Roberta, my then girlfriend, who's working in England for the summer. Her photograph, blown into a poster, fills half the wall above my bed. I don't need to look twice to see the influence of Bowie on the way she dresses, on the way her hair is cut, on the pose she struck when the picture was being taken.

The phone is ringing on the landing outside my door, so I go to answer it, not forgetting to take my keys with me this time – once locked out, never forgotten.

The man's voice on the other end asks for the young woman who lives in the downstairs flat overlooking the seafront.

'I'll check if she's in,' I say, smiling to myself. I've already left two notes with phone numbers on her closed door, each from a different man. The notes are still in place, so I assume she's still out but I knock anyway. No reply.

'Sorry,' I tell the man when I get back to the phone. 'She's not in at the moment. Can I leave a message?'

'Ehm... no... I'll ring back in half an hour if that's ok?'

'Sure thing. I'll be here.'

'Thanks,' and the phone clicks dead.

Out of habit, I press button B but no money appears in the return tray.

'Worth a try,' I say out loud and then go back to my flat to finish the letter.

On the small table, Roberta's most recent epistle, and some poems she's sent, lie beside a pile of singles. My small record player has run out of batteries; otherwise, the radio would be off till later in the night. George Harrison is singing "Give Me Love." I go on writing, my almost indecipherable scrawl covering the pages. I'm in love with and in awe of Roberta. She's a year behind me in college but ten years ahead of me in maturity. Whenever we're together I seem to be on edge, yet the summer has dragged without her. I know my sense of inadequacy has nothing to do with her. It has everything to do with my lack of belief in myself. Ask me to stand in front of a thousand bellowing students and address them, rabble-rouse them, lead them on a march and I'll be on to it like a shot. Indeed, that's how Roberta and I met, at a student occupation in the college at Earlsfort Terrace.

I don't know whether it's my perception of her sophistication, her much broader experience of the world or simply my inability to believe in myself once the audience has gone home, but I do know that I find myself much more comfortable with keeping the relationship going by letter than face to face.

I go back to the letter I received from her that morning. *You always said I make you feel uncomfortable. Is that why I haven't heard from you this week? Anyway, please get in touch. Every time the phone rings in the office, I hope it might be you. Sometimes I think it's what gets me up in the morning. I wondered if I should tell you this when you rang last week but, of course, I didn't. We never tell each other what we should. I think we never say what we need to say, what we're feeling, do we? Two stubborn sods.*

I smile at that, at the idea that a call or a letter from me might be the highlight of her day. And at the admission that I'm not the only one who keeps his feelings under wraps. I sense the concern in her words.

What I don't know now is that by the middle of October the Simon Park Orchestra will be at number one with "Eye Level"- I'll actually see them on *Top of the Pops* in Roberta's house as our *grande affaire* falls apart. Noel Edmonds will introduce this bunch of middle-aged men in their orange shirts and she'll sigh, the way she does when she wants to let me know something is boring her but is too polite to say. And I have no idea that this relationship will mellow into a deep, important friendship; that this friendship will carry me through some dark days and that by the end of 1989 this vibrant, beautiful, mischievous young woman will be dead. Not knowing this, I try, as well as my twenty-year-old self will allow, to tell her how much I love her and miss her and how I'm looking forward to seeing her in September.

And the phone rings again and I step out onto the landing to answer it. The same man who called before. My tap on the downstairs door goes unanswered; the notes are still in place. No, he doesn't want to leave a number and he's sorry for disturbing me. He'll try again in an hour or two.

Twenty minutes later, when I walk to the post box on the corner to post my letter to Roberta, I notice the curtains are drawn shut on the window of the downstairs flat. But there's nothing new in that; I've rarely seen them open.

That night, sometime after eleven, there's a quiet tap on my door. It's the young woman from the flat downstairs. She's wearing a short skirt, knee-high boots and a white blouse. In her hand she holds a sugar bowl.

'I'm sorry to disturb you,' she says. Her accent is midlands English, her tone is warm. 'Would you have some sugar, only I forgot to buy some earlier and I've got a caller who takes sugar in his coffee?'

'No problem,' I say. 'Come in.'

She stands just inside the door. I go to the cupboard and find a bag of sugar and pour some into the bowl.

'You've got lots of records, I see,' she says.

I nod.

'Who's the girl on the poster?'

'My girlfriend. She's working in London for the summer.'

'She looks beautiful.'

'She is.'

'Oh and thanks for leaving the notes on my door. I hope the phone calls are not driving you up the wall.'

'Not at all.'

'And thank you for the sugar.'

'Any time.'

Years later, I'll see this young woman's photograph in the newspaper and suddenly everything will fall into place – the phone calls; the notes; the closed curtains. I'll read the article beneath the photograph, an account of a trial, and realise she's been murdered by her pimp.

Father

I wake in the night and, for a moment; I have no idea where I am. Then, in the half-light of the moon I see the familiar architecture of the bedroom and I smile. I think of the lads' room in Abbeylands; of myself tucked up in my bed; of my father lying on the other bed; of his telling the story I never tire of hearing.

'It was a cold, wet, windy night when I left Castledermot on the bike. I was doing night-duty at the time. This was long before ever we got a car. And I had to be in Athy for ten o'clock, to let the down train through. Anyway, when I got to Kilkea Bridge wasn't there a big, black bull standing in the middle of the road. I got down off my bike and sized up the situation. I had to get to work and this fellow showed no signs of moving.'

'So what did you do?' I asked, already knowing the answer.

'I thought about it and then I struck on a plan.'

'What was the plan?'

'I took off my rain cape and I waved it about. The bull snorted and stamped his hoof. So I moved a bit closer and he snorted even louder. Pawed at the ground, lowered his head, getting ready to charge.'

'What happened then?'

'I moved to the side and he turned to face me. I waved the cape a few more times and down went the head and he charged. And, just as he got to the cape, I flicked it aside and he was going that fast that he went straight through the wall of the bridge, into the river and was swept away. And I put on my cape, got up on the bike and went on to work.'

And I thought of the many evenings when we crossed that bridge on our way from Athy. I'd look at the stones that had repaired a break in the wall of the bridge and I'd ask: 'Is that where the bull went through the bridge?' and my father would nod: 'It is, the very spot.'

Son

It's the late summer of 1974. My friend, Richard Ball, and I are living in a tiny flat on Palmerston Road in Rathmines. We're working the nightshift in the Hallmark card factory. Just the pair of us and an Englishman, called George, in the vast night-time factory, the German language Christmas cards rolling off the sealing machine. We gather them in bundles of twenty, box them, seal the boxes and store them at the end of the factory floor.

As the day-shift workers arrive, we take the early bus back to Rathmines and bed down for a couple of hours sleep. In the afternoons we kick a ball in Palmerston Park or go into the city to see a film or just sit in the overgrown back garden and read.

The flat is tiny, half a room. As we climb into bed in the mornings, we can hear the man in the flat next door get up and cook a fry. We know this because we can not only hear but smell the cooking through the flimsy wall that divides one apartment from another. The flat is a temporary arrangement for us, sub-let by my friend Pat Clowry who is away travelling for the summer.

By the beginning of September I have three job offers. I attend an interview at the Canadian embassy for a job at a First Nation school in Alberta. Then there's an offer of a job at a convent school in north London. The third is at the Vocational School in Castledermot, my home village.

I take the third.

Years later, I will wonder why I chose one above the others. Partly, I know, it was the call of home but, partly, it must have been a fear of the unknown; an unwillingness, then, to walk through whatever pathless woods my steps would have taken me? And partly it was some sense of responsibility. Easy to be a dreamer, more difficult for me to be the person I would like myself to be.

Father

There was the night, I was no more than eight or nine years old, when Mick O'Neill came visiting, as he often did, and stayed for supper, as he often did. We had recently moved to the new house on the High Terrace from the older house on the Low Terrace but the flat-roofed back-kitchen hadn't yet been built. The foundations and some of the block work were in place but the cooker was still housed in the small kitchen that also served as a living room.

Mick O'Neill was a regular visitor and a nicer, kinder man I've seldom met. He lived just two doors down from us but he'd often wander in at nine or ten o'clock at night and stay till the small hours. My father would *hit the hay* no later than eleven or nod off in the armchair in the corner of the room, his snores interrupting the conversations about politics and local goings-on. Mick and my parents were members of the Labour Party and, later, when it was pointed out to my father that, as he said himself, *We hate to lose you but we think you ought to go*, Mick moved with him into the world of independent politics.

But on this winter night, my father was wide awake and he was discussing the road works that Mick was overseeing out near Knocknagee. My mother was busy at the kitchen table, laying plates and cups and cutlery for supper. Five minutes earlier, as she plugged in the kettle, she had put an apple tart in the warming-drawer of the cooker. Now that the tea was wet and the table set, she turned to me.

'You can take out the apple tart,' she said. 'It ought to be nicely warmed by now.'

I slid the drawer open and there was the apple tart and there, sitting on the crusty pastry was a startled mouse. I had inherited my mother's dread of mice, so I slammed the drawer shut.

Grabbing a hurley stick from under the stairs, my father undertook to deal with the situation, with Mick's help, while my mother and I retreated to the safety of the hall. From there, we could hear the cooker being manhandled out from the wall and then a deal of banging and knocking, followed by a loud, muffled thump, a silence and then my father's voice calling urgently: 'Una, Una, can you come in here quickly.'

Inching the kitchen door open, my mother and I were met with the sight of Mick O'Neill stretched on the kitchen floor. It seemed to me that he was dead but my father quickly reassured me that he had merely fainted. My parents manoeuvred him into a sitting position, as far from the blazing fire as possible, and slowly he came round, my father spooning brandy between his pale lips. Only when he was fully recovered did the story emerge.

Mick, it turned out, was as unhappy in the presence of mice as my mother and me but he hadn't wanted this to be known so, when my father asked him to help in locating and disposing of the little creature, he had quietly agreed. Once the two men had pulled the cooker away from the wall, the mouse made a dash for freedom but my eagle-eyed father, hurley in hand, connected with the little fellow and sent him into the next world with one whack of the stick. The deceased mouse flew through the air and down the open front of Mick O'Neill's shirt and the unfortunate man fell in a faint on the floor.

'And where's the mouse now?' my mother asked.

'Disposed of,' my father said. 'I took it out before I called you.' And then he turned to the wan and palely loitering Mick. 'I didn't want you passing out on me again.'

I was thinking of this story as I drove to the hospital to visit my father. It was mid-January 1999, a cold, wet night, and I'd left behind a mousetrap set, beneath the floorboards of the kitchen. A mouse had found its way in and, over the previous week, I'd set a trap each morning and night and, always, when I checked, it had sprung but, in doing so, the metal clasp had caught the floorboard and the mouse had escaped. My father, I thought, will have the answer. He had always been a dab hand at catching mice.

At the hospital, I ran through the teeming rain, and made my way along the quiet corridor to the ward where my father and two other retired railwaymen lay, like rusted, decrepit engines in a forgotten siding – one hundred and forty-one years of rail work between them.

After we'd talked for a while, I explained the mouse situation to my father. 'If you have any bright ideas,' I said, 'I'd be delighted to hear them.'

He looked at me, his tired head on the barely hollowed pillow, his eyes dim and dull. When he spoke, it was as if his voice was that of a stranger, coming from another place and time.

'Every living creature wants to stay alive as long as it can,' he said. 'Nothing wants to die.'

Son

I've never liked New Year's Eve – too much forced jollity; too much looking back in disappointment at last year's failed resolutions; too much looking forward in an attempt to not be the person I am.

The Christmas of 1974 brings the usual excitement. I love Christmas, I always have. I love the sense of anticipation; I love the carols; the lights; the cards; the shop windows; the bustle; the music at midnight Mass; the feeling that all is right with the world, that we're not a bad species after all. Mud are top of the charts with "Lonely This Christmas" (and I'd never have imagined that I'll record the same song twenty years later with Gerry Ryan, Joe Taylor and an Elvis impersonator for an album by The Three Old Men in a Pub) but there are other songs knocking around the top twenty that are more to my taste. Ralph McTell has the "Streets of London"; Elvis is singing a cover of a song originally recorded by Richard Harris called "My Boy" and Rod Stewart and the Small Faces have a song called "You Can Make Me Dance, Sing or Anything (even take the dog for a walk, mend a fuse, fold away the ironing board, or any other domestic shortcomings)."

The days after that Christmas bring a crash. A current girlfriend informs me – after I've given and she's accepted my Christmas gift – that she isn't giving me anything for Christmas because she isn't going out with me anymore *as of right now* and, yes, she is sorry I've bought those tickets for the New Year's Eve disco and, yes, she'll be happy to find someone to go with her. Years later she confesses that she'd taken her new boyfriend to the disco and years later I confess that I'd known she would.

So there I am, footloose and frantically wondering what the hell I'm going to do to get myself through New Year's Eve. I could stay at home with my parents; I could take off to a local dance in Carlow or Athy; I could travel to Navan and spend it with Richard Ball, or I could just go to bed and sleep through it all and wake to the first day of 1975.

Instead, I ring Roberta, tell her the situation and ask if she has anything in mind for the last night of the year.

'Not a thing,' she says. 'I'll probably watch TV. I think the folks are going out. Feel free to come up if you like.'

I catch the evening train from Athy to Dublin; the bus from town to Terenure and I'm in her house by ten.

'So, what would you like to do?' she asks.

It's a cold, clear, frosty night.

'We could walk,' I say.

'Sounds good. Let's do it.'

And off we go, following the course of the Dodder, walking and talking. The finer details of the conversation have slipped away but there's an ease between us as we chat. There's little left of our romance of three years earlier but, instead, there's forbearance and an acceptance that was never there when we were going out together.

We talk about Bowie and Carole King and Leonard Cohen and Paul Simon. We talk about college – Roberta is in her final year, I've just graduated. We talk about what we hope to do with our lives and where we hope to go. And I realise, perhaps for the first time in my life, that it is possible to be lovers and, later, friends.

We walk and walk and somewhere in the distance bells ring out the old year and ring in the new but we hardly hear them. And, finally, we reach the sea at Ringsend and then we turn and walk back the way we've come. Into the small hours, the noise of the New Year celebrations growing fainter as the city finally retires for the night; getting back to her parents' house beneath a sky already lightening with the imminence of the new dawn.

'This was the best New Year's Eve I've ever had,' I say as we stand in the hallway. 'Thank you.'

'It was wonderful,' she says quietly and she kisses my cheek. 'And, now, let's have some coffee. I'm frozen.'

Brother Ghost

All these photographs of you, from infancy to death's door. I look through them and I remember or I don't remember when they were taken. Many date from way before my birth.

You, standing in the garden, short trousers, wellington boots, a sword in one hand – the Pirate King even then – the other holding Dolores' hand. You're in the shelter of an apple branch. It must be spring, the buds are on the tree but not in blossom. What age are you? Eight or nine? You're looking bravely into the camera, small sister by your side.

Or this one – you and me sitting on the bonnet of the old Ford in the driveway of the house on the Low Terrace. I'm two or three, you're twelve or so. That was the car in which you learned to drive, the car you reversed into the gatepost when our father was away. I was four years old by then and you put me standing on the back seat and warned me to give directions so you could reverse out through the narrow gate. Who knows what went wrong. You'll say I wasn't concentrating, I'll say you weren't concentrating. Either way we'll laugh.

Or this one. You and me on the big swing in the backyard of the Low Terrace and you're there with your arms around me, hands holding me firmly, both of us smiling into the dazzling sun, our shadows on the scuffed earth beneath our feet.

Or this, my favourite of all the photographs, taken maybe a year later. The three of us: you, Dolores and myself. We're standing on the swing this time. You at the back, the tallest of course, smiling broadly but looking a little sheepish. Dolores in the middle, in a colourful summer dress, white shoes and socks, nine years old or thereabouts. And me in my white shirt and dungarees; chubby-legged and still knock-kneed, which might explain the heavy boots in summertime. Behind us, in the distance, rise the houses of the High Terrace, which will, in a couple of years, become our new home. But, for now, we are here, smiling and happy and the sun is shining on our lives.

There's one more, of you on a tricycle, the tricycle I inherited and used until the seat collapsed and it was thrown onto the flat roof of the shed in the garden of the Low Terrace, *until it can be repaired*. It was still there when we moved house. Our father, as you know, was a great gardener but a handyman he was not – just like you, just like me! His response to any urging from our mother to try some repair work was: 'There are people to do that sort of thing.'

In or around the time when that tricycle collapsed I had a birthday. It must have been my fifth because we had moved house by the time of my sixth. I'd been warned by our mother that there wouldn't be a birthday party that year – which was most unusual – and all I saw was the unfairness in the decision so I invited several of the boys in my class to our home, without telling her. And they duly arrived, presents in hand. I don't remember the party – no doubt she cobbled something together quickly, she always did. But that night there were harsh words.

Only years afterwards did you point out that she may have been ill, may have been going through hard times. I had no idea, but I was not about to be denied my party and, more importantly, my presents.

Father

I look back now, from the experience of my own darknesses and the way they have driven me to run from life, from love, from relationships, from those who cared and care for me and I recognise in that running a mirror image of my father's darknesses. We were never close enough to talk about the memories he carried of his childhood and adult lives but now I believe I have some sense of the regret, the loneliness and the anger he must have felt at the opportunities that passed him by. The chances for a happy childhood, for continuing education, for promotion in his workplace, for a possible career in national politics – stymied by the internal machinations of a political party – all of those possibilities that failed to materialise across the years.

He was never a man for articulating those regrets but they may well have driven him to seek solace and camaraderie among the men with whom he drank.

His pride in our success was real but can have been little comfort in the face of the breaks that passed him by and might, had life been kinder, have opened paths he would love to have walked.

Son

One of those house makeover programmes is on TV – a sixties bungalow being brought up to date. There are shots of the rooms before the builders start swinging their sledges and the kango-hammers begin to root out the floors.

In one of the bedrooms there are two single beds, one on each side of the room with a dressing table between them and behind it a window looks out over a garden. But it's the covers on the beds that catch my attention, the two candlewick bedspreads with their raised embroidery patterns, the ones I remember from the room Jarlath and I shared.

In the corner, its back to the unused fireplace was a wardrobe and, at the foot of my bed, behind the door, sat an enamel bucket that appeared in late summer, half filled with water glass. Into this, over the weeks and months, my mother would deposit eggs that had been bought while prices were reasonable, eggs for the Christmas cakes. Their winter scarcity made it wise to gather them earlier in the year and preserve them for use when the time came.

But it was the bedspreads, with their raised pink flowers, that led me back through the open doorway of memory, to stand, again, in the lads' room. To lean through the open window on a summer night; to ask Jarlath why he was laughing as we read our books late into a winter night; to half-wake in the small hours of a night after Christmas as he stole, quietly, in from some party or dance in Carlow or Tullow; to feel that all was safe with the world for now.

I watch as the builders clear the house on TV. The owners pick and choose the pieces they wish to keep for what will be their revamped home. What to keep and what to throw away? Everything else goes into a skip in the yard.

But memory doesn't work that way, memory makes its own choices beyond our say so.

Brother Ghost

I was never sure and I still can't say I know, even now, quite what your relationship, or mine, was with our home village, that village that liked to call itself a town. When I write town you know I'm talking about the hurl of streets and lanes that make up the village where we were born and grew up and will be buried.

This is the place where our mother taught all her working life; where you taught for three weeks; where Dolores subbed on and off; where I taught for six years. This is the town that has grown out around the edges but suffered heart-failure at the core. This is the town where the centre has been left to fall down while houses proliferate on the periphery, in what were fields. A town – like so many others – where the centre did not hold.

This is the town where Peter Murphy kept us entertained in the Castle Cinema; the town where Joan of Arc stood life-sized on a pedestal in the garden of *La Pucelle*, the Aylmer family home; the town where we went to school; the town I loved; the town I wasn't so sure you were enamoured of; the town with which we had this perplexing relationship; the town where half your ashes lie; the town where – so the Postmistress, Carrie Murphy, told me – I have to be buried, *Sure where else would you go? It has to be here.*

This is the town where, in your youth and mine, there was a bakery; a haberdashery; a clothes shop; six or seven grocery shops; half a dozen pubs; a pair of butchers' shops; two newsagents; a tin-roofed bookies; three garages; a Post Office; two cobblers; a barber; a couple of hairdressers; a doctor's surgery; two banks; four schools; two football teams; a coachbuilder; a hardware shop; an undertaker; three churches; a monumental works and a dozen tradesmen to deal with any problem that needed solving.

Now there's a shining new community centre, a beautiful coffee shop and floodlit sports pitches, but so much else has gone. Parts of Main Street and the village Square are derelict beyond belief. You don't see it and I'm sure you wouldn't want to, even if you were alive.

This is the town where our mother is buried. You flew home from the States to see her before she died. And then you were away, back to the hospital where you worked. A week later she was gone. We spoke before you left.

'She won't recover,' you said. 'Don't make any major changes in your life for at least a year after she dies.' Brotherly advice.

This is the town where our father is buried. I remember that long walk to the church from the funeral home, in along the Mill Road, past Kelly's house and the football field; stopping briefly at the gate of the house that was home to us from 1958; then on past the Middle Terrace and the Low Terrace, where we three survivors were born; through Carlow Gate and up to the Square.

'We should really stop for a minute's silence outside The Pig and Whistle,' you said as we passed Gannon's pub – a favourite haunt of our father – then down Main Street and into the bright, refurbished and newly decorated church.

That night, sitting in the kitchen, you suggested I should be the one to say *the few words* after the funeral Mass. Dolores nodded. I was surprised. You were the elder son, always the more eloquent in my opinion, more urbane, more charming; more assured.

'Wouldn't you like to say something?' I asked.

You shook your head.

'I'll do one of the readings. You're the writer.' I waited for you to add: 'You're the poet,' but you didn't. Like *the dead arose*, one of your favourite ways of addressing me was *Well, poet?*

But that night, sitting at the big kitchen table, I saw a different side of you, someone less assured, less comfortable in our home town. I recognised in you the very uncertainties that were and still are there in myself. Where did that come from? From being the teacher's children? From being the children of blow-ins? Or is it just an innate uncertainty, a lack of confidence?

Was it because our parents, like Stephen Spender's, tried to keep us from children whom they perceived to be rough? I don't have the answer and neither, I think, did you.

'Maybe you could sing after I've spoken,' I said.

You laughed.

'You could sing "Golden Days."'

You laughed again.

How I wish I'd asked you to sing it then and there, sitting across the kitchen table, the January fire burning low in the pot-bellied stove, for Jack, for me, for us.

Golden days, in the sunshine of a happy youth.
Golden days, full of gaiety and full of truth
In our hearts we remember them all else above
Golden days, days of youth and love.
How we laughed with the joy that only love can bring.
Looking back through memory's eyes,
We will know life has nothing sweeter than its springtime.
Golden days, when we're young.
Golden days.

Son

It's a morning in the summer of 1978. For whatever reason, I'm up and about just after dawn and I take the dog off for a ramble over the fields. Nothing unusual in that. Across the Little River – a stream that can be negotiated in a stride but where, as children, we had fished for pinkeens. On we go, along the banks of the River Lerr, its clear water catching the earliest rays of the stretching sun.

This is the river where Michael O'Neill and Liam Mulhall and I had tried – one November – to catch trout in sacks. Wading into the two-foot depth of freezing water, we had used an improvised net, made from a coal sack and a length of wire, and tried to lure the unseen brown fish from the overhang of the bank into our badly-designed and hopelessly ineffective trap. An hour later, all we had caught were colds.

But on this morning the river is already warm with the season. A light mist hangs over the water at the Back River, a dammed three-foot-deep pool where, as a ten year old, I had tried, unsuccessfully, to master the art of swimming. Thirty years would pass before I was able to manage a dozen tentative strokes.

On we go, the dog nosing ahead of me, drawn by the elusiveness of rabbits and foxes, through The Rocks – a sprawling wilderness of granite boulders, furze bushes, reeds and secret hiding places where cowboys camped and Indians laid ambushes for them. The place where one of my childhood friends was stripped to his shorts and staked out, by a warring tribe who promptly forgot all about him so that, by the time his brothers found him, dehydrated and terrified in the late afternoon, he was severely sunburned.

Crossing the stone bridge at Halfmiletown, we loop back onto the Barrack Road, passing the Mill Pond, drained now. The same pond where, as a three-year-old, I was placed in that tin bath and sent out to sail on the deep, black waters.

But, on this early summer morning the tin bath, the heavy jute sack, the days of pinkeen fishing are long, long gone. I'm a teacher now, working in the local vocational school. Teaching children, who have, themselves, swapped the fascination with pinkeens and fishing and adventures in the Rocks for the lure of the Friday night hop in the youth club and the sound of Blondie, Bob Marley and Showaddywaddy.

And on we go again, the dog and myself, down into the village and back home. The sun is well clear of the horizon by now, the shadow of the house lies stretched on the lawn between the rose bushes. The dog rambles ahead of me, into the back yard, in search of water and food. I stand at the gate, watching the last of the mist evaporate above the lazy fields.

And then I hear it, the deep, raspy sound of a corncrake coming from somewhere out on Murphy's farm. The sound is distant but not too distant, there like a lure, like a rainbow – just across the next ditch or the next fence, always within reach but beyond touch. I know well enough not to set off in search of the bird, I know well enough to stand and listen to the raw, throaty song that goes on and on across the open sky. What I don't know is that I will never hear that song again, that the corncrake will never reprise his music in that part of Kildare and that I am privileged to hear what I am hearing.

Like so many other things in life – pinkeen fishing, tin-bath sailing, cowboy and Indian adventures – there comes a day when we step away, without knowing that we will never go back, we become that *someone* of whom Dennis O'Driscoll wrote so heartbreakingly.

But on this summer morning we share something, the corncrake and myself, a last song, a few moments of sunlight when the world is ours and ours alone, a farewell that goes unrecognised and, as a result, unacknowledged and uncelebrated.

Brother Ghost

Our father often tucked me into bed and, as he did, he'd say: *I think the sandman is coming, me ould segotia.* And then he'd lie on the other bed, your bed, in the lads' room, and tell me that story. Always a version of that story to do with the railway and the bull on Kilkea Bridge. Did he tell you that same story when you were a young boy?

And then he'd fall asleep and his gentle snoring was a comfort to me and, shortly afterwards, I'd fall asleep myself, that warm and loving phrase in my ears, *me ould segotia.*

You had names for me, too, names that sang of the closeness between us, names that reminded me that you'd always be my older brother, the bigger, the wiser, the more optimistic of the pair. Even, in adulthood, when my eyes were level with your own.

You didn't call me *segotia* but you had these other nicknames that I loved to hear, not for the sound or the sense but for the warmth that came with them, the reminder of good days long gone.

My good man. You brought that one home from your first summer in England. You'd gone there to earn your college fees, working in Walls' ice-cream factory – or was it canning peas that year? The occasional letter came, with its British stamp. And Friday after summer Friday I traipsed to the Post Office with our mother's weekly letter and the local paper, *The Nationalist and Leinster Times*.

Years afterwards, a local woman who had grown up in a poverty-ridden family in the village talked to me about that summer and how she'd been on a tube in London when you got on with your friends and how you sat beside her and talked to her.

'I didn't expect that,' she said. 'I mean, ye were reasonably well-to-do people and we were dirt poor and I didn't expect him to reck me, let alone sit with me and introduce me to his student friends.'

And I thought of the petty class system of the village we grew up in – the public reading of the Christmas and Easter dues in the local church. We got two Sundays entertainment out of it – the long list of contributions, starting with the local GP and the garage owner and their £10 each. Down through the farmers and teachers (including our mother who would scrape the dues together, even in bad times) to the labourers and shop-assistants, each in their place in the financial pecking order, labelled by their ability to keep the ship of church afloat. And pride ensured that even those who were on the poverty line scraped together their shilling or their sixpence. And, by spreading the ordeal over two Sundays, there was a differentiation in itself. If your name was relegated to the second Sunday you were among the also-rans.

But that September, when you got back from London with your black and white photographs of you and your friends, dressed in white, industrial suits with white hats, standing at conveyor belts or lounging in the London sun, you called me *My good man*, putting on a mock-English accent and I laughed and I loved it.

The following summer you were in London again and The Rolling Stones were playing there but that was never really your kind of music. You loved Mario Lanza and *West Side Story* and Mozart – always Mozart.

And that year, 1962, when you came home in September – for a couple of days before college opened – you called me *Squire*. That was the one that stuck. Others came and went, *Young Man* and *Loo-lah* among them, but *Squire* stuck and I had a fondness for it. I saw myself as your shield-bearer, your armour-carrier, just as I saw you as my Knight. When you arrived back from England or when you landed home from college for Christmas, you brought calm and possibility. I stopped worrying. I didn't have to be the intermediary any more. I was no longer the ten-year-old boy seated at the kitchen table, one parent at either end, trying to get them to talk, trying to think of some topic of conversation that would bring, even for a few minutes, an agreement, an end to the silence that always threatened to explode into harsh words.

I admired the way you seemed unaffected by it all. And you weren't afraid to wade in and sort them out, tell them what you thought of the incessant skirmishing, badger them into good humour or at least into a truce. I could never do that. Instead, I was the eternal go between.

Years later, when we talked about it, when I told you how much it meant to me to have you in the house and how much I dreaded your return to college, you laughed.

'It was down to age, Squire. I didn't take any bullshit and, I suppose, they treated me more like an equal because I was that bit older.'

But I wasn't convinced. It seemed to me that there was something in your personality that allowed you to face up to things, deal with them head on, while I tended to try to be the pleaser, not rocking the boat, going with things *for a quiet life* to use a phrase both parents claimed from time to time, though I can't say I ever noticed their quietness.

It was a Christmas in the early sixties when I finally got to hear Tchaikovsky's 1812 Overture. That was the Christmas of the big snow. The weather changed in the last week of the old year and by New Year's Eve a blizzard was blowing across the east of Ireland and Castledermot was wrapped in a deep, stinging harshness of white. But, on Christmas Eve there had been no sign of the snow and you had arrived on the last train to Athy, your Christmas holiday work done. And not only had you arrived home but you'd brought a gift for the family – a record player.

No sooner were you in than you were gone again but half an hour later you were back with an armful of LPs – borrowed from the local butcher and singer and actor, Frank McDonald. And there among them was Tchaikovsky's 1812 Overture.

We sat enthralled as you led us through the music and, though I felt I already knew it and could tell what was coming next and why, so contagious was your passion that I said nothing. I heard the cannons roar, I heard the church bells ring, I saw the troops advance, I watched them in retreat and, by the time the last notes died away, I felt as if I'd sat through an epic picture at the Castle cinema.

'Now that's music,' you said.

And later, as I drifted to sleep, with one ear open for Santa, you came into our room and I wanted to say how brilliant the music had been and how great it had been to hear you talk so knowledgably and so keenly about it but I didn't. And you said: 'Night, Squire.'

'Night.'

'Sleep tight. Don't let the bugs bite.'

Son

I'm preparing for a run of James Plunkett's *The Risen People*. During rehearsal time, I take down a red flag from the rafters in the garage to use as a prop in the play. It's a flag that has been lying there for years, a flag that had been draped over one of my father's election posters on the Square in Castledermot when he left Fine Gael and joined the Labour Party. The red flag and a jacket turned inside out. We had been on our way to Mass one Sunday morning when he spotted them. He stopped the car, removed the jacket and flag and went about his business. The jacket he used later to start a bonfire; the flag went into the rafters of the garage. He won that election to Kildare County Council.

As I take the flag down that evening for the play rehearsal, he remarks drily: 'It'll be interesting to see if any of the cast recognises it first-hand!'

I wake one night in late January to hear my father on the phone to Dr Dyer, our GP. Going into my parents' room, I find my mother in excruciating pain.

'It's my head,' she says.

I dab some 4711 Cologne on her forehead.

'That's better.'

'The doctor is on his way,' my father says and he sits quietly on the edge of the bed.

Five minutes later the doorbell rings and the doctor is on the stairs. I step out of the room while he examines my mother.

Downstairs, I plug in the kettle and throw two briquettes on the dying fire. The kitchen is filled with the warm smell of a freshly baked apple tart. And then I hear Dr Dyer in the hall, ringing for an ambulance.

'I believe your mother may have had a stroke,' he tells me. 'You might keep an eye out for the ambulance. I told them you'd put on the outside light,' and he's gone, back upstairs. I follow him, go to my room and pull on my jeans, a jumper and a pair of shoes.

Outside, the night is cold. The light from above the front door throws shadows along the lawn and they meet the shadows thrown by the street light across the road. I open the gates at the end of the short driveway. The street is empty; a three o'clock silence sits on the brow of the hill at Mat Neill's house. At the other end the dark, empty shape of Kelly's shop squats against the deeper darkness of the countryside beyond.

From my parents' room upstairs, the dull light of the bedside lamp muzzles through the bedroom curtains. How many nights have I come home from dances at this hour, and later, to see the same light shining? How many nights have I stepped quietly into the kitchen and caught the warm and wonderful smell of my mother's baking. But now the porch light, the hall light and the street light meet and blend, making a kind of day of the darkness. I kick a stone across the road and a woken bird flies up from a tree in the plantation – the narrow belt of evergreens that shelters us from the open countryside beyond the football field.

And then another light shatters and circles in the sallow lights of street and house – the flashing sapphire of the ambulance as it creeps along the row of houses that is Abbeylands – our street, our neighbourhood, our home. I flag it down. My cousin, Peter Smith, leans from the driver's window and smiles.

'Una?' he asks.

I nod.

'We'll back into the drive.'

The wide doors thrown open; the stretcher on the stairs; Dr Dyer issuing directions; my mother, pleased to see Peter, urging him not to drive too fast; my father seated at my mother's side and then the closing doors, blue lights again, along the street and disappearing down Carlow Gate. Only when I turn to address the doctor do I realise that he, too, has gone and the empty garden and the open door and the vacant house beyond are mine and mine alone for now.

That afternoon, when I get home from teaching in the Vocational School, my father is in the kitchen cooking dinner. The news from the hospital in Dublin is that there is no news.

We sit at the dinner table and eat.

'Would you like a cup of tea?' I ask, after we have finished the meal.

'Might as well,' he says.

I put the cups and plates on the table and plug in the kettle. Opening the warming drawer of the cooker I see the apple tart my mother baked the night before. I take it out and put it on the table. We sit in silence, the tart there between us. Neither one is willing to cut it, as though that act might desecrate a memory.

'Maybe we'll have it for supper,' my father says.

My mother dies four weeks later, in late February. As her funeral cortege arrives at the village the streets are lined with a guard of honour of children from the National School where she had taught for forty-four years. We bury her in Coltstown cemetery, the last of the winter winds battering the spring afternoon on the side of the little hill that, incongruously, raises the burial ground above the surrounding countryside.

Twenty-two years later, on a dark, damp evening in January, my father dies in the local hospital in Athy. He is a few days short of his ninety-first birthday. Dolores and I have spent most of the previous days at his bedside while friends and family come and go. On this evening, I go home to get some rest. Just after seven the phone rings.

'Get here as fast as you can,' Dolores says.

I drive like hell through the empty streets of the town. When I reach the quiet room in the hospital, where my father has been moved, the priest has just finished the prayers of the Last Rites. Dolores, my cousin Peter and his wife, Anna, and my stepmother, Debbie, are sitting around the bed.

'John is here,' Debbie says into my father's ear and then she turns to me. 'He held on for you.' I take my father's hand but I know he's already dead.

'You must be Jack's brother,' the priest says.

I burst out laughing.

'Must be the wear and tear,' I say. 'I'm his younger son.'

There are so many changes in the twenty-two years between those funerals. Marriage to Mary; the births of our two children; changing jobs; moving house; separation; divorce; moving house again; meeting Caitriona and then moving house again and again. My parents' coffins sit in my memory, like bookends to that part of my life.

Father

Yes, I have the paraphernalia that contain a life between my parents – the birth, marriage and death certificates; my mother's rosary beads; my father's wallet; a shell from the twenty-one-gun salute fired over his grave; his watch, stopped now; his penknife, that knife I watched him use to sharpen pencils on the steps of the railway signal cabin; a handkerchief; a bar of Turkish Delight chocolate I found in his pocket – the wrapping says *Best Before Nov 99* – solidified now with age.

I knew my father, of course I knew him. I was forty-six years old when he died and yet when I think about memory, and what we recall of our lives and the lives of others, there's so little about his life that I really know.

There are all the odds and ends that are missing, so much he never spoke about. I picked up bits and pieces across the years, in throwaway comments, in the conversations of others, in the empty spaces in photograph albums. About his childhood – losing his mother shortly after childbirth; being taken away from his home as an infant, to be looked after by an already overworked grandmother; returning home when his father remarried, only to lose his stepmother to death within a short time and then being raised by his older sister, Lal, who became mother and, later, housekeeper to her siblings. There was the crowded cottage, the shortage of money, the dreams of education which were buried beneath the need to work and pay his way. None of this was ever spoken of. My father was not a man to dwell on the negatives; he was never given, to quote himself, to *that class of thing*.

'There's enough suffering in the world without bringing any more of it down on ourselves,' he told me once.

His life reminds me of those lines of D.H. Lawrence: *I never saw a wild thing sorry for itself. A small bird will drop frozen dead from a bough without ever having felt sorry for itself.* Yes, there was a self-sufficiency about him, a shortness of temper in his younger days but he mellowed as he grew older. He seemed incapable of feeling wretched for himself. He never once used the losses of his childhood as an excuse or an explanation for any of his failings, though it might have clarified things if he had. Life was how it was; it washed things up on the shore and then the waves receded; there was nothing to be done about any of this, so it was best to just get on with it.

Now and then a sentence would stumble out that betrayed something buried deep beneath. A saying for which he had a fondness was, *Let the last hour be the hardest* and he wasn't one for romanticism but then that's hardly surprising.

And if he had his faults they were far fewer and less damaging than my own.

Brother Ghost

Do you remember the day of Dolores' wedding? You and Clare were staying in a country house, halfway between Athy and Castledermot. You had the flowers for the buttonholes. Don't ask me why but you'd collected them the night before and we were less than an hour from the wedding time and there was no sign of you putting in an appearance. Me being me, and me being best man, I was a like a hen on a hot griddle.

No mobile phone, no contact, no knowing what was delaying you. And when, with fifty minutes left and a short fifteen-minute drive ahead – *oodles of time*, you'd say – you arrived, I had a go at you – about how fine you'd cut it, about the fact that we were all under pressure. You said nothing. Not like you to let it go, to not defend yourself. You hadn't been feeling well, Clare said. So I backed off. Realised how stupid I was being. We'd still be at the church with half an hour to spare.

Was that the beginning of it all, of the illness that would scythe your life? Hard to tell at this remove but it's something that has haunted me ever since.

Father

What was it that kept us physically apart? I was looking at him in his coffin, ninety-one years of life and living; his face still twenty years younger than it ought to be; the hair still wisped across his head but the sparkling eyes so firmly and so finally closed.

I touched the back of his granite hand, the ridges of a lifetime of physical work still there, raised in the veins that tracked beneath his skin. I wanted to kiss his forehead, run my fingers through the greyness of his hair, feel the wintriness of his cheek against the warmth of mine but it was all too late. I had never hugged my father in my adult life and there wouldn't be another chance. His body lay small but stiff between the walls of his coffin.

'Your father would want something decent, something good,' Jim Dunne, the undertaker, had said and I'd known he was right. Though he wasn't much given to thinking or dwelling on death, my father was always resolute about his appearance. The buying of a new suit – something that happened every couple of years – was a major event that took time and several visits to M. G. Nolan's outfitters in Athy. It wasn't death that would have interested my father but, rather, the importance of not appearing shabby. This last and wooden attire might not be what he'd ever wanted to be seen in, much less to have thought about but, even if it was beyond his control, he trusted it would to be up to scratch.

And so I watched him, nestled there, the soft white fabric tucked beneath his head, the dark wooden walls already closing in on him; the smell of timber and death in the air. We had shaken hands so many times in recent years, laid hands upon each other's shoulders; patted one another on the back.

I'd kissed his forehead during the dozens of hospital visits but we had never hugged.

I'd put it down to his reluctance. I'd chalked it up to his childhood losses. I'd told myself it was all ok, that these things didn't matter. But standing there in the funeral home, my brother and sister standing beside me, the friends and neighbours filing by, I knew I'd been lying to myself.

My brother and he had hugged; my sister and he had hugged. The reticence had mostly, but not exclusively, I believed, been mine. The tacit fear that had sat between us went back to years of infighting, years of distrust, years of wariness. But in that moment I wished I'd been the one to back down, to put my arms around him and hold him closely – his chest pressed to mine. I wished I'd buried my face in the rough warmth of his jaw, felt his heart beating if even in my imagination. But here he was – heart stopped, face cold and angled, breath gone wherever but, certainly, for ever.

Son

To look into the years to come, to take that step into the frosty Christmases and the soft spring evenings and the high summer days and foggy afternoons is to make an act of faith – in the future and in the past. Without the future there is no hope and without the past there is no memory. Without memory and hope there is little point in the now.

Here in St James' cemetery I am surrounded by the monuments which mutter of the past and promise a future. I am part of the aftertime these tower-builders and stonemasons and dead shopkeepers and labourers and children dreamt about.

One of the things I longed for in childhood was to have roots in this village. I spent so many afternoons methodically checking the headstones for a name that might have meant I had an ancestor buried here. Where else are there deeper roots than with the deep rooted bones of our families. That is the truth of the land. Those bones become the living sinews of the places we call home. I think of my parents, my stillborn brothers, all part now of this landscape, unseen fragments of an ongoing existence.

I can stand on the moonlit side of Rice's Hill and look up, into the breadth of space, at the dark places between and beyond the stars, and know that, in spite of everything, I have my place in the world and I can truly call it home.

To have a place that is home is to have a place from which to look forward. To glance at the possibilities to come is to imagine the changed, the altered. I envisage the old cinema levelled; fields swallowed by bulldozers; houses that once were homes with their empty windows gulping in the winter winds. I look back at an old Super-8 cine film and the winding, narrow Main Street I see is just a memory now.

But the future teems with energy, new lives, optimism. On other, deep December nights, people will gather here. On summer evenings, children will play on the lanes and, if their occasional glances should fall on my chiselled name on an angled stone, I don't expect that gaze to linger too long because life is for doing, for being in, for enjoying and discovering.

Those children will find their own hopes and aspirations and loves. They will suffer their own losses. They will survive. Life will not be kept down and laughter will not be smothered. New faces appear behind shop counters. New hands are rested on the plough. New feet race to the shops on Christmas Eve. New eyes gaze out in wonder at the night sky.

In their remembering we, too, may have the echoed half-chance to live and smile and laugh again, to bid each other the greetings of a season until the end of time.

Brother Ghost

We were walking on the beach, an early morning in high summer: the Atlantic breakers rolling in from the east; the sun high and hot; the sands dotted with families; the waves lifting and dropping body-boarders in the warm shallows.

'Let's walk to the channel,' you said and we did.

The talk turned to our parents and what it was that had brought this unlikely couple together, the schoolteacher, born in Sligo, growing up in Galway, and the railwayman, born in Laois, growing up in Carlow and Kildare.

'I never understood it,' you said, 'chalk and cheese.'

You talked about your memories of our house as you were growing up and I talked of mine and although our experiences fell ten years apart they echoed each other.

'I used to wish Jack would carry through on his threat to go back to England and work there,' I said. 'I thought life would have been a lot more peaceful at home. The thought of the scandal of it at the time never worried me. Even as a ten-year-old, it seemed to me the wise thing for them to do, to go their separate ways.'

'I never could figure what it was that attracted them to each other in the first place.'

'Politics? Didn't they meet at a political dance?'

You nodded.

'Hard to imagine what else it could have been. Well, politics and tennis.'

'Politics is not necessarily the greatest love potion in the world,' you said and you were laughing.

'Do you remember it as being bad when you were growing up?'

'Good days, bad days. More so when I was in my teens and twenties. There always seemed to be that tension in the house.'

'You can sing it. That's why I always looked forward to your coming home. I felt safe. I felt you'd take control of things. You seemed to be able to handle them. Not to take them as seriously as I did. You let the arguing and the bickering roll off your shoulders.'

'Did I? Maybe I did.'

'You did.'

'Maybe I just had more practice at it, a lot of the time. It was a bloody nightmare.'

'Well – all I can say is that I was really glad to have you there.'

'Thanks, I hadn't realised that.'

We walked on, the sea pounding to our left, the sand warm beneath our feet, the sky above a deep and settled blue.

'It's an awful thing to say but life became calmer after they died.'

You nodded again and we went on walking. I don't know what you were thinking but I was regretting, even then, the time spent in worry and uncertainty during my boyhood, time I would never get back and time I would never forget. Those days of despondency – for that is what it was to live in that house at that time as, effectively, an only child – still hung over me and go on hanging over me even now.

Son

I'm sorting some CDs when I come across Judy Collins' album *True Stories and Other Dreams* with its superb song "Secret Gardens of the Heart" and those wonderfully evocative opening lines: *My grandmother's house is still standing, though it isn't the same*.

Every time I hear those lines, they take me back to my own grandmother's house in Church View in Tuam, that solid, early twentieth century dwelling, built for my train-driving grandfather, Tim Bray, and his wife, Brigid McHugh, after they moved from Sligo to the smoky Galway town. And the things I remember most are the details of the yard outside the back door, an enclosed area that led through a rose-scented arch to the fertile, rambling garden which backed onto the cattle mart. Beyond the mart, the spire of the Church of Ireland rose into the sky and gave the house and the road on which it was built a name.

In the yard was the low turf shed that smelled of summer all year round, the warm, peaty scent trapped between the timber walls and the genuflecting roof. Its floor was soft beneath the feet. Fifty years of turf mould had tempered the earth, making it pliable and welcoming each time I stepped into the musky twilight to fill the turf basket for the range that heated the large kitchen and cooked the food we were about to eat.

Outside the door of the shed was a bottomless wooden barrel, in which – or so my grandmother told me – kittens were regularly drowned. Only in my teenage years did I realise that there were no cats about the place and that the warning was simply a ploy to keep small children away from the danger of dying in the soft rain-water gathered for hair-washing.

But the thing I remember most vividly is the headless statue of Blessed Martin de Porres – he hadn't yet attained sainthood in those days – that lurked on the sitting room windowsill, his head resting beside him on the painted timber.

'Why does Granny keep that statue when it's broken,' I'd ask my mother but the answer never came. Instead, I'd be told to run and play and warned never to ask that question of the woman herself. Not that I'd dare. Brigid McHugh was a small woman but she was feisty. Sharp was a word that well described her. She was mostly welcoming and sometimes kind but Church View was her ship and she ran it by her rules.

In the long summer days, I played in the shadow of the headless Martin, catching his sideways eye from time to time, wondering why someone hadn't tried to fix him, tempted to glue his head on backwards, just to see if anyone would notice, but knowing I never would.

Years later, I think around the time my grandmother died, I heard, at last, the full story of the statue.

One of my aunts had been taken seriously ill in 1959 and my grandmother had prayed to Martin de Porres for a cure, a man to whom she had a huge devotion and a man in whom she had total faith. But the cure never came and her daughter, still a young woman with a very young family, died.

When the news came, my grandmother, in a fit of anger and desolation, flung the statue against the sitting-room wall, smashing the head from the body. Later, regretting the fact that she had blamed the hapless (and headless) Martin for her daughter's death, she put him on the back window of the sitting-room, his head beside him but facing away from her, so that whenever she entered the room she didn't have to meet his gaze – a kind of compromise of exclusion that didn't cast him into external darkness but left him with a lot to think about.

When Martin was canonised in 1962, the promotion went unrecognised in Church View and he sat, still headless, still facing away from those who very occasionally entered the best room.

And here I am, west of the Shannon, driving through the winding streets of Tuam. I park the car, get out and walk the perimeter of my grandparents' garden. House and garden are much changed now but I imagine my grandmother among the flowers and I think of summer days in the yard, watched over by the statue, and Judy Collins' lines come to mind, about ghosts bending and sighing in the kitchen. And no doubt the deepest, saddest sigh of all is my grandmother's, for the loss of her youngest child.

Father

Occasionally, out of the blue, my father would tell me a story from his young days. Like the one he told me one evening as we drove home, about the man who lived on a busy street in Athy.

'This fellow had a reputation for being a late sleeper so one night, on our way home from a concert, myself and some of my friends tied a black ribbon to the man's door and placed a card beneath it – for all the world like a death notice.

'The lines on the card read: *Neighbours, neighbours, do not weep, he is not dead but fast asleep*.

'The card and ribbon remained in place till the fellow finally got out of bed late the following afternoon. All day long it drew the attention of people passing by. They'd stop to read the sad news but go away laughing.'

He laughed at the memory and I laughed with him.

Brother Ghost

Granny Bray was a tough woman. What she said went. I liked visiting Church View. I loved the pink roses that dripped from the arch above the gateway into the vegetable garden. I loved the broad-leaved rhubarb plants that were shelters from the rain, the sound of the drops magnified as I found refuge beneath their wide, green shield, pretending I was in a jungle in deepest Africa.

I didn't love the outside toilet with that nine-inch gap at the top and bottom of the door, that gap where a mouse once ran in and did laps about the base of the bowl before running out again, while I sat petrified beneath the naked forty watt bulb.

I don't think you were as fond of the place as I was but, then, by the time I remember holidays there, you were in your late teens and early twenties and out and about with our cousins, Tim and Declan and Anne and Jane. And, later, all of you lot ended up in medicine of one kind or another, veterinary or human.

Granny Bray was strong on rules and the nightly curfew was one of her favourites. It seemed to give her that feeling of power, that control over who came and went and when and where. I was never brave enough to challenge the curfew but you were!

There was the night when she sent you on your way to the pictures with the usual strict warning that the doors would be closed – *and locked* – at eleven o'clock and anyone who didn't make the curfew could *sleep in the turf shed or find other accommodation of their own choosing*. You were in our cousins' house in Brownsgrove, playing cards, and it was well past one in the morning when you faced the locked doors – front and back both firmly bolted.

The choice was clear: turf shed; the long walk back to Brownsgrove or finding a way past the keeper of the keys. Luckily for you, our Aunt Bridie – who nursed in the midlands, the same aunt who gave us money and cigarettes and let us drive her car when no one else would – heard the gentle rattle of gravel on her window pane and sneaked downstairs and let you quietly in.

But then you were faced by the vision on the stairs. Granny Bray standing on the landing staring down at you and Bridie, her long, grey hair – normally tied in a neat bun – falling around her shoulders and down her back; her ankle length nightdress completing the rebirth of Miss Havisham. She was not pleased and let you both know in no uncertain terms that you were lowering the tone of the house and *what would people think*?

The tirades continued the following day but you had done what hadn't been done before, and never would again: you had broken the curfew.

Father

There's a *rath* near where we live, one of thousands scattered across the countryside. As we grew up, *raths* or fairy forts were places to be avoided. There was something about them – a stillness, a history and an inkling of something dark and deep, something not to be disturbed.

We were warned, time and again, that these precious circles of earth and grass and thorn trees were the homes of the Little People. We were cautioned that any interference with them could bring only misfortune and heaven knew what else. And so, crossing fields, we skirted them for the most part and, if one of our gang did venture into the sacred space he – it was always a boy – would be called back and reprimanded for his foolishness.

And then, one morning in the summer of my seventeenth year, I was walking home from a dance. I had missed my lift and dawn was breaking, the soft mist lifting slowly from the fields, hanging like the remnants of ghosts around gateways beyond which the crops were slowly ripening.

On a long, straight stretch of roadway, I saw a cyclist in the distance, pedalling slowly towards me. As he passed, we bade each other a good morning. It was only then that I noticed the spade tied along the bar of his bike and the small cardboard box bound securely to the carrier.

It was my father who gave the explanation later that day, telling me that the man was taking a stillborn child to be buried in a *rath* not far from the road where we'd met.

'It's what some people do,' he said. 'On account of their not being allowed to bury the unbaptised child in consecrated ground. And some people bury the children in the ruins of old churches.'

What he didn't say then and what I wouldn't know for a further seven years was that he had buried our stillborn siblings in the wild patch at the end of our garden. It was something he would talk about only once and then with the proviso that it never be spoken of again.

Decades later, my sister, Dolores, would tell me of how our mother had cried bitterly when we left that house in 1958 and moved one field away to a newer and bigger house. She was leaving more than a house and a garden behind.

And now, when I pass the *rath* near our home in south Carlow, I think of the other Little People – not the musical, dancing fairy folk but the countless dead children whose only music is the sighing of the wind in the winter branches and whose only recognition is in the small rises within the larger, deeper mounds of clay and grass. And I raise my hand in greeting and in memory of my own siblings, buried forever in memory.

And I think of my mother shedding those tears on that bright July afternoon more than sixty years ago and I think of my father explaining the reason why that early-morning cyclist was going about his sad task and I understand his silence about his own children lying quietly at the bottom of our garden.

Brother Ghost

You called and said you were having some tests, that you hadn't been feeling well. You said the tests were extensive, that they were trying to rule stuff in and out. You said it might be one of dozen things. We talked about Paddy, your parrot, and I asked whether your illness might be something transmitted by birds.

'Could be,' you said.

And the weeks passed: emails; phone calls; updates. Still nothing sure; nothing definite or, if there was, you weren't saying. And then, one afternoon in the early summer of 2005, I answered the phone and it was you. Clare was on the other line.

'Lou Gehrig's disease,' you said.

'What's that?'

'It's known as Motor Neuron Disease in Europe,' Clare said.

It didn't ring any immediate bells with me.

'Three to five years,' you said.

An icy perspiration ran down my back and arms and my forehead was immediately clammy. I sat down at the kitchen table.

'Bastard,' was the best I could manage.

'You said it, Squire. That just about sums it up.'

The rest of the conversation is a blur. Clare put the best spin she could on things and we talked about the fact that we'd already been planning on travelling to America in July.

'I can come over earlier if you'd like,' I said.

'Not at all. We'll see you in July.'

We said our goodbyes and I hung up. Caitriona came from the kitchen where she'd heard half the conversation. I knew, by the expression on her face, that I must look a wreck.

'Bad news,' I said and I told her the story you'd told me. 'I don't even know much about the bloody thing.'

I Googled the disease. It didn't make for easy reading. The full horror of the diagnosis dawned on me and something burst over me like the slap of a heavy wave.

'I have to talk to someone about this,' I said.

'Of course.'

'It's fucking unbelievable.'

'I know. I'm so, so sorry this is happening.'

'John Macdougald,' I said. 'I have to talk to John.'

'Do. Go on, go now.'

Outside, the sun was shining. I sat into the car and did nothing, just sat there wondering what you were doing in those minutes. Were you making other phone calls? Were you sitting stunned in your living room? Were you walking the shores of the lake beside the house?

A warm wind blew through the open car windows. I started the engine but it cut out. I turned the key again and drove slowly down the avenue. Into town, between the unhurried cars and lorries, down the Crib Road to avoid the worst of the traffic, past the teenagers lying on the grass in the park, left at the church and into the empty car park of the medical practice.

The surgery was closed but the door was still unlocked. Inside, the waiting room was deserted. Susan Braithwaite, the surgery receptionist, was shutting down her computer in the office.

'The surgery is closed,' I said.

She took one look at me and must have guessed something was wrong.

'Take a seat in the waiting room. I'll get John.'

In his room we sat and talked. John explained the details of the disease to me. The facts. The timescale.

'There's no good news I can give you with this disease,' he said. 'Nothing I can say that will make it any better.'

He was cool and he was calm and he was compassionate, as ever. He was just who I needed. We discussed the family. Holly, Jarlath's daughter, had spent some time with him a few years earlier, during her medical training. He talked about fear and about dealing with it.

'Does the disease run in families?' I heard myself ask.

He told me about the chances of that happening. We talked for a long, long time and when I was leaving, he put his hand on my shoulder.

'I'm sorry,' he said. 'I'm really sorry. And I'm here, any time – day or night.'

Back home, Caitriona told me that Dolores had been on the phone. It was her husband Peter's birthday and they were on their way to visit us. When they arrived we talked. She wondered if we should travel to the States immediately.

'I don't think so,' I said. 'If it was me, and you and Jarlath arrived at my door, I'd be expecting the undertaker right behind.'

We agreed to see how things might go in the coming months. Caitriona and myself would be travelling in July. Dolores and Peter would travel later in the summer.

That night and the next day and the rest of that week were an ache in the pit of my stomach. I wanted to call you but I had no idea what I could or would say that would help in any way. And, I imagined, the last thing you needed or wanted was someone like me with some mealy mouthed cliché that meant little because it could change nothing.

It was like being back on the stairs in Castledermot, listening, waiting. But this time the voice I was waiting for wasn't the raised voice and the words weren't the words of anger, though anger was what I was feeling. This time the voice was the voice of death, the words in my head were those of the old Latin hymn:

Dies iræ, dies illa
Solvet sæclum in favilla,
Teste David cum Sibylla.

Days of wrath and days of mourning... heaven and earth in ashes ending.

I woke in the middle of the night and, for a moment, I imagined it had all been a nightmare. For a few seconds I thought about the summer trip we'd planned: driving to Charleston; walking the beach; going to a basketball game; hanging out; talking about the past; looking to the future; being brothers in arms.

Outside, the night was stuck fast but I got up and went downstairs and put Leonard Cohen's CD *New Skin for the Old Ceremony* on in the study and listened over and over to "Who by Fire." I'd been rehearsing a show of that name when our father died in 1999. And here I was, six years later, listening to the same music, knowing your death was looming.

I found a copy of a prayer from the Jewish Day of Atonement, the prayer on which the song is based, and I sat in the lamplight and read it, searching for some consolation. But all I found was the certainty that, like in the children's game, ready or not, here came death.

On Rosh Hashanah it is inscribed
And on Yom Kippur it is sealed
How many shall die and how many shall be born
Who shall live and who shall die
Who at the measure of days and who before
Who by fire and who by water

Who by the sword and who by wild beasts
Who by hunger and who by thirst
Who by earthquake and who by plague
Who by strangling and who by stoning
Who shall have rest and who shall go wandering
Who will be tranquil and who shall be harassed
Who shall be at ease and who shall be afflicted
Who shall become poor and who shall become rich
Who shall be brought low and who shall be raised high.

Next morning, I talked to Caitriona about what I'd heard and what I'd read.

'There must be more positive ways of looking at things,' she said.

'Maybe.'

I spent the morning in my study, trying to write something, anything, but nothing came. I wanted to mail you words of hope, of consolation. Words. Words. Words. That way, if you wanted to ignore the written word, you could ignore it.

I looked through my CD collection, searching for something that might give consolation. The best I could find was Pete Seeger's "Turn, Turn, Turn," his interpretation of the passage from Ecclesiastes.

There is a time for everything, and a season for every activity under the heavens: a time to be born and a time to die, a time to plant and a time to uproot, a time to kill and a time to heal, a time to tear down and a time to build, a time to weep and a time to laugh, a time to mourn and a time to dance, a time to scatter stones and a time to gather them, a time to embrace and a time to refrain from embracing, a time to search and a time to give up, a time to keep and a time to throw away, a time to tear and a time to mend, a time to be silent and a time to speak, a time to love and a time to hate, a time for war and a time for peace. What do workers gain from their toil? I have seen the burden God has laid on the human race. He has made everything beautiful in its time. He has also set eternity in the human heart; yet no one can fathom what God has done from beginning to end. I know that there is nothing better for people than to be happy and to do good while they live. That each of them may eat and drink, and find satisfaction in all their toil – this is the gift of God. I know that everything God does will endure for ever; nothing can be added to it and nothing taken from it. God does it so that people will fear him.

But, in the end, words are only words. They lift, they sadden, they flatter, they flummox but they don't have it within them to change things. But you know this; who knows it better?

Son

'You should ring Jarlath and talk to him,' Caitriona says. 'See if he'd like you to come over sooner rather than later. See what's best for Clare and him.'

So we talk again. A couple of days have passed since the initial call. I suggest travelling to the States soon and lending a hand in whatever way I can.

'Further down the line,' Jarlath says. 'Further down the line will be when I'll need you more, when things begin to fall apart. I'll pay your fare.'

'No you won't. If you do, I won't come,' I say and we both laugh, as though death is somewhere beyond the furthest horizon we can imagine. It's the first time I've laughed in days.

'But not yet, maybe in the autumn you could come out for a longer time,' he says. 'Let's wait and see how this thing pans out. We can chat about it in July.'

On 2 July, a Saturday, I drive to Sligo with my cousin David Smith to watch Kildare play Sligo in the All-Ireland football qualifier series. It's a dirty, wet, cold day and, crossing the Shannon, I get an uneasy feeling, not just about the match – being a Kildare supporter means living in a constant state of uncertainty, anyway – but about everything, about life and the months and years that lie ahead. And the game itself doesn't raise the spirits. We lose 1-11 to 1-10 in a dour, dogged match. The drive back is a morose affair.

Two days later, Caitriona, her son Eoin, and I fly to America. Ironically it's 4 July, a day of American celebration and razzmatazz. At Dublin airport, we buy some last-minute presents – books and a CD and a sweat-shirt for Jarlath. I don't know what else to get him. I'm lost and anxious and uptight.

A few days earlier, Holly had emailed us some photos of Jarlath and a caution – if that's not too strong a word for it – that we might be surprised at the changes in how he looks:

Hello,

I was just in NC over the weekend and took some photos of Dad with my friends' baby. I thought it would be helpful for you to have seen the changes in his appearance over the past few months. John, if you have a difficult time opening them, the last two are of just him.

Dad's on the oxygen all the time -- Mom and I tried to get him to sometime use another machine to better open his lungs, but it keeps him from sleeping. He has problems sleeping well in general and can easily begin napping if nothing's going on. Mom helps him to the bath, but he can make it up and down the stairs on his own. Lou Gehrig's is a hypermetabolic illness, so he has continued to lose weight -- mostly in the form of muscle mass. Mom's doing her best to add calories into his diet with butter, ice cream, etc. Dad's speech slurs a bit when he's tired. At times he gets behind in the conversation, but as my friend Jim said, that just allows the rest of us to catch up. He's the same person. And his spirits are good. Mom's being amazing keeping everything together.

I left a book on Lou Gehrig's with the parents that you can look over when you're here. Mom also scheduled an appointment at the clinic for when John's in town.

I'm glad you both are coming. He's really looking forward to seeing you. I'm bringing Madison to NC when John's up, and I'm arranging a flight to be in town when Dolores arrives.

Let me know if you need any info, etc.

I'll see you soon.

Be safe until then.

Love,

Holly

In the photographs, Jarlath looks more or less the same as ever. Yes, he has lost some weight and, yes, he's wearing an oxygen feed in his nose but it's the same brother, grinning at the camera, the same boyish look in his eyes, the same devilment behind the smile, the same brother I've loved all my life.

Brother Ghost

Coming through Raleigh airport terminal, I thought again of the first time I'd landed there. Back then, you'd been the one coming to meet us, your smile was the first smile we'd seen and you were the one who ushered us, over-laden luggage trolleys and all, through the automatic doors where everything was the reverse of the world we'd left behind. Here, the air that hit us as the doors slid open was hot and summery and a huge moon was hanging in the deep Carolina darkness. Tonight there was just the very last trace of the waning moon, a sliver of light in the night sky.

Clare was there to greet us and to bring us the news that you'd been hospitalised with a slight infection but you'd be out again in a couple of days. On the way to the house, I spoke with you on the phone and you said you'd see me next day and that all was well and you were glad we'd made it safely across the pond.

The following morning Clare drove me down to Wake Med hospital, less than a mile from the house. I sat in the car, the air conditioning on (your laughing words, from the last time we'd driven together in Carolina and I'd opened the window instead of turning on the air con, ringing in my ears:

Mother Ireland, you're rearing them yet) as we drove out of Pebble Loch Lane and turned right onto Glen Echo Lane; then right again onto Kildaire Farm Road, the trees stretching their shadows in the morning sun. We stopped at the lights and, as we waited to cross Tryon Road, I glanced down to TGI Friday's and Walmart off to the side – places we'd gone with you – and then the lights changed and we crossed the intersection and turned left into the hospital grounds. I reckoned it was a twenty-minute walk and, already, I was thinking, come autumn, when I planned to return, the midday temperatures would be down to the 70s and, if you spent any time in the hospital, it would be a short and pleasant walk to be with you.

Clare parked the car and I followed her to your room. And there you were, up and about. The three of us chatted for a while and then she left us to it, to give us time to chat and catch up.

'This is a really shit situation for you,' I said. 'I'm really, really sorry.'

You nodded.

'You probably don't want to talk about it right now.'

'Not really. Tell me, what's been happening on Paddy's green shamrock shore?'

You sat on your bed and I filled you in on the news from home. We talked about the previous weekend's football defeat for Kildare. I asked how Duke was doing at basketball.

'Better than Kildare,' you laughed.

The television was on in the background and you pointed to the presenter.

'He used to be on CBS. I don't know if you've ever seen his show.'

I shook my head.

'Let's see what's on the other channels,' you said and you pointed the remote. Nothing happened. And then I noticed. You'd pointed it at a painting on the wall.

'Are you tired?' I asked.

'I am.'

'Maybe you should get some rest.'

'Yeah, I probably should.'

I put some pillows behind your head as you lay down, pulled the covers over you and turned off the television.

'I'll be here,' I said.

You nodded.

'Are you ok?' I asked.

You nodded again.

'I've packed some things for the journey,' you said and then you shut your eyes.

Something wasn't right about your breathing; something wasn't right about the way you looked. Something wasn't right. I called a nurse and he called another and then a doctor arrived and I was asked to step outside. The next half hour was spent on the long corridor, walking up and down, figures coming and going and then the doctor was at my side.

'It's not good,' he said. 'We're going to call Clare and have her come over.'

All through the afternoon we sat with you. I drove Clare's car back to the house to give Caitriona an update. I had something to eat.

'I might spend the night at the hospital,' I said.

'You should,' Caitriona agreed.

Late that evening, I drove back the short distance. There was just a hint of a moon in the sky. Elton John was singing "Daniel" on the car radio...*my brother, you are older than me...the scars that won't heal*.

'I'm going to stay,' I told Clare.

'Are you sure?'

'Yep, I'm sure.'

'You'll call if anything changes?'

'Of course. Will you let the kids know?'

'I already have. Robert and Holly and Sean each spent a weekend with Jarlath at the beach over the last couple of weeks. And his friend Bob Carper spent a weekend there with him, too. He was prepared for whatever might come. Once I'm home, I'll get in touch with Dolores.'

And so I sat with you that night, 5 July 2005 into 6 July, there in that small hospital room. You were asleep in the bed and I sat in the chair by your bedside. We were back in *the lads' room* again. Your lungs were opened and closed by machinery; your nose and mouth covered by a mask, for all the world like a 21st-century Jesse James. I began to write in the small notebook I had brought with me, the shadow of my hand falling over the blank then darkening pages. Much like yourself, I thought, with the shadow of illness and imminent death falling over you, *the scar that won't heal*.

I thought back to all the times you'd come to my rescue: the loans; the supportive phone-calls; the laughter; the advice; the times we'd spent together in Ireland and the States; the emails of encouragement, and now I wanted to be there for you as you'd always been there for me. More than anything I wanted to reassure you, as you'd so often reassured me that everything would be alright. You were the one who'd always found the solutions to the problems; you were the one we rang with medical questions; you were the one who got through or round difficulties; you were the one with the answers but there was no answer to this.

Several times during that night I told you I loved you. Outside, the slivered moon retreated by degrees. The nurses came and went, bringing coffee and biscuits. A couple of times a doctor called and I stepped outside. And, each time, as I was recalled to your room, the doctor said: 'No change.'

'How long?' I asked.

'Difficult to tell. Not more than a few days. But it's impossible to be sure.'

The laboured breathing went on – as our mother's breathing had gone on. My pen moved across the pages. I drifted in and out of sleep. I closed my eyes and I heard the echo of your words, your laughter. I wished we could be back again, reliving the days together – the football matches; the horse-play in the garden; the Christmas dinners; your arrivals home; the life we lived and the time I never valued deeply enough.

Early in the morning Clare arrived, followed by Bob Carper.

'You go on home,' Clare said. 'Get some rest. I'll call you if there's any change.'

Back at the house, Caitriona made me some food. I lay on our bed and fell into a deep, blank sleep, dreamless. Once or twice I thought I heard the ringing of the phone but it may have been my imagination. And then Caitriona was standing over me, her hand on my shoulder. In the instant, I was wide awake.

'Clare called. She said we should come.'

The five minute drive that seemed to take for ever. The hot, sunny carpark. The cool, clean corridors. Bob and Clare standing outside your room door.

'He's gone,' Clare said.

The body we saw twenty minutes later was already becoming a waxen copy of who you were. The breathing had stopped, the mask had been removed. The chaplain said a few words. And already I missed you like hell.

Son

What happens when someone close to me dies? I go into organisational mode and so it is when Jarlath dies. Clare and I visit the undertaker. Caitriona gets things organised in the house. I buy a new pair of jeans and a pair of shoes and a shirt for the funeral. We had travelled with summer clothes; we travelled in the expectation that this would be a holiday.

'You won't need a jacket,' Clare says. 'It'll be way too hot.'

The house fills up with family – Holly and Robert and Sean, Jarlath and Clare's children, and their partners and children. Dolores and her husband

Peter arrive from Ireland. I email some friends back home to let them know what's happened. The things we do now in these situations, the new rituals that replace the old. No longer do we tell the bees. Instead we email and Facebook the news.

And then the food begins to arrive from friends, from neighbours. That was something I had thought happened only in Ireland but, no, the food keeps on coming, just as it does back home.

'Would you write something for the funeral Mass?' Clare asks.

'I'd be honoured.'

I go down the street, to Louise Meminger's house and sit at her computer and type some words that grow into lines that grow into paragraphs.

As we leave the house on the Monday morning, 11 July, for the funeral Mass, I notice the small flagpole, two doors down, from which a University of North Carolina State flag usually flies. The Tar Heels are great Duke rivals and were spoken of only in the most dismissive and derisory terms by Jarlath, a Duke fan through and through. This morning the neighbour's flag flies at half-mast. It's a simple and much appreciated tribute from a basketball rival.

At the church, the pews are filling. The morning sun pours through the stained glass windows, dipping the seats and the altar in a wild palette of blues, greens, oranges and reds.

And, when the time comes, I speak the words, my brother's ashes and photograph resting on a table before the altar.

'When I was three, I was taken from my home by three thirteen-year-old boys. They put me in a tin bath and launched me onto the local mill pond.

The bath was controlled by a rope tied to the handle. The bath might have turned over. I might have drowned. For the boys it was an experiment. One of them was my only brother, Jarlath.

'When I was ten and living in the modest semi-detached house that was our home, a young English woman arrived at the front door. She'd met an Irish student in London. He'd given her a photograph of the nearby twelfth-century castle of the Fitzgerald family, telling her he lived there and, if ever she were in the area, she should call. Obviously, he didn't think she'd make the trip but she did and was politely redirected to "the local village" where she found our house. That student was my brother, Jarlath.

'The reasons I tell you these stories is twofold. Firstly, to confirm what you all knew, that Jarlath loved "chancing his arm." Secondly, to remind you that the last few months of his life were not what Jarlath was all about. He faced his illness with a patience I never guessed he possessed and with a bravery we can only admire.

'The village Jarlath, Dolores and I grew up in, Castledermot in Co Kildare, was a tiny place with a population of less than six-hundred people. There was an incredibly close sense of community in that place, a sense that I've seen reflected here in Cary in the past week. People have called; food has miraculously appeared; what has needed to be done has been done. Friendship has been manifest.

'And people have talked about Jarlath: about the joy they saw on his face as he listened to a string quartet; about the passion he had for Duke basketball and Coach K. Maddy has worried about who will now wind the cuckoo clock. Each caller has had a story of a good deed done, a word here, a favour there, a life well lived.

'It's been thirty-five years since Clare and Jarlath left Ireland but he carried a love of the country with him. I don't know if you knew but, before studying medicine, he qualified as a teacher and taught history for all of three weeks. He may not have liked teaching but he maintained his love of history.

'Indeed, he loved many things: Clare and their family and Duke; music and Duke; horses and Duke; Mozart and Duke; the smell of incense and Duke; Latin and Duke. The motto on his hospital desk said it all: *Illegitimi non carborundum* was, however, probably not picked up in his Latin class.

'Just ten days ago, I met a farmer in Castledermot. I told him I was coming to see Jarlath. "The great thing about the Doc," the man said, "is that he never forgot where he came from or who he was. He was always one of us."

'The last thing Jarlath said to me, on Tuesday afternoon, was: "I've packed some things for the journey." Among the things he packed were our respect, our friendship, our gratitude and our deep, deep love.

'There's an Irish saying, a prayer really: Codladh sámh agus suaimhneas síorai – it means, A sound sleep and eternal rest. It's what we all wish for and what we wish for Jarlath.'

I almost make it to the end and then my voice begins to go and I feel Robert's hand on my shoulder and I take a deep breath and I finish what I have to say. And then Robert speaks about his father.

'In years to come, anthropologists will wonder at the cluster of men called Jarlath in North Carolina. What they won't know is that so many grateful parents named their sons after the gynaecologist who saw them through often difficult births. But the parents will know and we will know. Let the anthropologists go on wondering.'

Later that evening, when most people have left the house and dusk is falling, I sit in the lounge and listen to the quietness. I see my brother coming down the stairs, as large as life, and my blood runs cold. And then I realise it's Robert – the image of his father.

A couple of days after the funeral, Clare suggests that Caitriona and I go to the beach house.

'I know you came to see Jarlath but this was supposed to be a holiday as well. If he'd been well enough we'd all have gone to the beach. You guys need a break, too.'

And so we take his car and drive from Cary to Emerald Isle, down I-40, three hours in the hot sun. I switch on the CD player, knowing the last time this car was driven on this road was by him on his way back from the beach. We listen to the music he listened to, the songs he inadvertently chose for us to hear. Hits from the sixties, when he was young and I was younger, a time when we both had so much to live for.

We pass the towns I drove past with him over the years. There's Auburn and Newton Grove, and Warsaw in the distance over there to our left. The rolling fields; the cars on blocks; the distant water towers; the towns that are shimmering mirages across summer fields are the same ones we noticed or didn't notice on our journeyings. And then we're on to NC 24E and the sun rises higher and the music plays. We pass Richlands and drive into

Jacksonville. The names are like a litany of lost adventures. We cross the New River, out onto Freedom Way and on to Swansboro. There's the Piggly Wiggly. We follow East Corbett Avenue and on to Cape Carteret and we're almost there. Bogue Sound to our left, the warm Atlantic waters to our right. And then we're at the summer house. Up the salty wooden steps and into the rooms we last shared with him.

That night we sit on the balcony and listen to the North Carolina buoys calling across the water, tolling the two syllables of his name, out there in the hazy night. I listen closely. There they are again. And again. Calling him or calling me. And the sea reminds me of John Masefield and John Masefield reminds me of his poem, *Vagabond*:

Dunno a heap about the what an' why,
Can't say's I ever knowed.
Heaven to me's a fair blue stretch of sky,
Earth's jest a dusty road.

Dunno the names o' things, nor what they are,
Can't say's I ever will.
Don't know about God – He's jest the noddin' star
Atop the windy hill.

Dunno about Life – it's jest a tramp alone
From wakin'-time to doss.
Dunno about Death – it's jest a quiet stone
All over-grey wi' moss.

An' why I live, an' why the old world spins,
Are things I never knowed;
My mark's the gypsy fires, the lonely inns,
An' jest the dusty road.

Brother Ghost

When we get back to Cary, we spend a few days with Clare. One afternoon when she and Caitriona have gone to the shopping mall, I go upstairs and step into your room. All the accoutrements of sickness are gone – the machinery of existence. But there, by your bed, are the last books you read: *Poems of Ireland* that Dolores sent to you and a couple of books on Irish history.

You, who were never coming back, came back vicariously in those last few days and weeks, back through the words and images to the places you had visited only as a tourist in the last thirty-five years of your life.

I sat on your bed and imagined your soul in a small coracle, crossing the Atlantic waters, making land on Inis Mór and resting there a while before it crossed the last of the choppy seas. And then I saw you, a pilgrim traveller, journeying east – through Tuam, stopping at the gate of our grandmother's house – and on and on across the midlands until the landmarks became familiar. Uncle Gerry's Bridge outside Portarlington; the walls of Moore Abbey in Monasterevin; the railway bridge in Athy where you paused to glance down along the line to the cabin where our father worked; then on through Bray and Grangenolvin and Kilkea and Mullaghcreelan until the chimneys of Castledermot rose between the summer trees and you were home, but there was no one there to meet you.

Son

We get back from the States in mid-July to a sun-soaked garden and building work that has been going on in our absence. The builder, Arnold Gee, has moved a rose bush that came from my parents' house and replanted it in the garden. I'm grateful – particularly grateful in the circumstances. Another man might just have bulldozed it into the ground.

And we come back to a car that sounds like a tank. I drive it for a few days and then take it to the garage. Despite there not being any sign of a leak, the oil has run low and the advice from the mechanic is to the point.

'I'd be getting rid of it as soon as I could. It won't be going anywhere for long without a new engine.'

Good days, bad days, I think.

Late one evening the following week the doorbell rings. Outside is a man from Castledermot, a man who had grown up with Jarlath.

'I just called to sympathise,' he says.

'Come in.'

'I won't, I'll just finish this cigarette and then I'll be on my way.'

We sit on the windowsill of the unfinished house extension and he talks about my brother.

'He was no great shakes at football,' he says. 'But he was clever, which was better.'

I nod.

'There was one time he got a football – I think maybe your mother bought it for him. He used to bring it down below to the football field and we'd all play. We'd pass it to him when we could, it was his ball after all, but he was never going to win an All-Ireland.'

He goes on talking, about other times, better times. He lights another cigarette and then a third.

'Are you sure you won't come in and have a cup of tea or coffee or something?'

'I won't. I'm just about to hit the road.'

He talks of schooldays and a particularly violent teacher.

'Oh tell me about it,' I say. 'I suffered under the same man ten years after ye did.'

'He could never really get Jarlath because he was bright. He went for the chaps that were a bit slower and he thrived on bullying and beating the weak lads – the poor fellows from out the country whose parents were in awe of him.'

Five cigarettes later the conversation winds down and we shake hands and the man drives away. I'm grateful for his having called and grateful for the stories he's told but the account of the football has stuck in my head because I already know that story from a conversation we had over the days of our father's funeral.

The football hadn't been bought for Jarlath. He'd earned the money himself, thinning beet. It was a leather football, an old-fashioned one with a bladder inside, laced up, but state of the art for the time, 1954. And, yes, he had organised matches in the football field and, yes, there were fellows who were a lot better than he but that didn't stop him playing. And one evening there had been a set-to between a couple of the lads playing in the field, nothing out of the ordinary, nothing that wasn't brushed under the sod in a couple of minutes but one of the boys marched off in high dudgeon, saying he'd *get* the rest of them.

Later, Jarlath had been kicking the ball against the shed wall as night fell and, when he was called in for supper, he left the ball in the garden and forgot about it.

The following morning, when he went to collect it from the lawn, he discovered it had been punctured half a dozen times, speared by the blade of a penknife. The stitching was ripped and the ball was beyond repair. Word on our little street pointed to a certain individual who lived elsewhere in the village. Word had it that this was his way of *getting back* at the team. Much was known but nothing could be proven.

Three weeks later, in the first days of August, I flick on the car radio, just as the death notices are being read on the local station. The third name on the list is Jarlath MacKenna. There I am, driving between the ripe fields of corn, ten miles from home, and news of his death is reaching me again. It seems like I'm in a coil, turning back on time. But, of course, the notice is for

Jarlath's second funeral, the burial of some of his ashes in the family plot in Castledermot.

The church of the Assumption is packed that Saturday morning, 6 August, a month to the day after his death. Hundreds of people cram the pews where we had expected a hundred at most – old college friends; medical colleagues; cousins; neighbours; men and women who had grown up with Jarlath, among them the man who reputedly had destroyed his leather football.

As I stand at the lectern to read a poem I've written for Jarlath, I have a vision of our father's coffin in front of the altar, Dolores reading Brendan Kennelly's poem "I See You Dancing, Father" and Jarlath on his way up to the lectern to read from *Ecclesiastes*, his hand lightly brushing the wood of the coffin lid.

I want to be back there and then, back to that time when he had six years of his life still left before him; I want to have all those days, all that time still to spend; I want to know that there will be days and nights in which to finish old conversations and begin new ones; times to tell him how much I love him and how much I depend on him; *time, time, time, see what's become of us*.

We walk to the cemetery, a mile to Coltstown, and Robert kneels and places the urn of ashes beneath the kerbing of our parents' grave.

'It won't be disturbed there for future openings,' Jim Dunne, the undertaker, had explained the day before.

'You mean when I'm put down?'

'We won't talk about that ... Just yet,' he laughed.

Prayers over, we walk back to the Schoolhouse Restaurant where they had expected eighty guests for the meal but where they feed 120. I can hear Jarlath chuckling in my ear, *The loaves and fishes all over again*. Friends reminisce, the afternoon shifts into evening, the laughter comes in waves as stories are told – strokes pulled in student days; good turns done for people trying to get work in America; advice passed down the phone; contacts made with medics here when things were moving too slowly.

'He never forgot his roots or who he was or who his neighbours were. You can't say better than that of a man.' We're standing outside the restaurant and the speaker is clasping my hands, his eyes locked on mine. 'If everyone remembered who they were and where they came from, the way Jarlath did, wouldn't the world be a much better place?'

'It would,' I say.

'It would indeed,' the man says and there are tears in his eyes.

A few weeks later, I pick up the local paper and I read something hugely uplifting, an article on my brother by the historian Frank Taaffe.

The Irish have peopled the English speaking countries of the world. The far reaches of what was once the British Empire have become a home to the Irish diaspora. Australia, New Zealand, South Africa but above all North America have been enriched by and in turn have enriched successive generations of Irish emigrants. Emigration was for the Irish of the 18th and 19th centuries, an escape from the poverty and disease of a downtrodden country. In the early decades of the following century, emigration provided a safety valve for many disillusioned by the aftermath of a war waged to regain a nation's freedom which subsequently degenerated into civil war.

In more recent years, we have become accustomed to describing the emigrant's impulse to leave the Ireland of the Celtic Tiger as "voluntary emigration." It's a flight from the country of one's birth motivated by desire to savour new lands, new sights and cultures rather than a reaction to the negativity of unemployment and the cultural stagnation of previous decades.

Whatever the reason, emigration has over the centuries claimed uncountable millions of Irish men and women. Whether from Athy, Castledermot or some other parts of Ireland, those who departed these shores seldom if ever returned. Death, when it came, arrived under a foreign sky and the mortal remains of those once young Irish men and woman today lie in scattered cemeteries throughout the world. Buried sometimes without ceremony, often in the absence of family and friends, the Irish emigrants were and remain a forgotten part of our country's heritage, that undefined yet unique element of collegiality and social interaction which makes the Irish people so special.

Sometimes, but only sometimes, the impersonal overseas burial rite for the emigrant is replaced by the generous send-off which is part and parcel of an Irish funeral. Last Saturday was one such occasion when family and friends of Jarlath MacKenna came together in the Church of the Assumption in Castledermot to pay their last respects to a man who had emigrated to North America 35 years ago. He was the eldest son of Una Bray, a Galway woman who as a young girl came to teach in Castledermot, and Jack

MacKenna, a railway worker for the Great Southern and Western Railway, later C.I.E. His mother died in 1977 and his father 22 years later and last Saturday part of Jarlath MacKenna's ashes were laid within his parents' grave following a moving ceremony in Castledermot Parish Church.

Jarlath had been ill for some months but his death when it came was unexpected. His son Rob, at the start of the church ceremony, spoke eloquently and kindly of his father, touching on his career as a physician, his devotion to his family and his loyalty to his Irish roots. The soloist, soprano Colette Boushel accompanied by Sr. Francis Jerome on the organ, provided a fitting hymnal background to the ceremony which was both moving and evocative of the spirit of an Irishman whose adult life had been spent in America.

A very special contribution to the church ceremony came when Jarlath's younger brother John spoke of a pre-arranged visit to Jarlath in America and of arriving there just in time for the brothers to spend one last night together talking and reminiscing about young days spent in and around Castledermot. It was a particularly poignant contribution made all the more so by John's reading of a poem he wrote that night, as life slipped away for his brother Jarlath.

The very personal valediction which speaks of a brother's love for an older brother was read in the Church last Saturday and made a deep impression on the members of the congregation. Jarlath McKenna is survived by his wife Clare, his daughter Holly, his sons Rob and Sean, his sister Dolores and brother John.

My heart rises, not just because of the kind words but because I know how proud Jarlath would have been – proud of the reception and proud of the warm and heartfelt recognition by his friends, neighbours and peers, a recognition he never seemed to believe he would receive in the land of his birth.

The first of the dreams is warped in time and place and there are five or six of them over the following weeks, all following more or less the same pattern. The initial dream comes sometime late in August, as the summer is taking its last, long breaths. I dream I'm back living in a cottage on the edge of Mullaghcreelan Wood, a place where I had lived from 1992 to 1994 – more than a decade earlier. In this and the dreams that follow, I'm in another room when the phone rings in the kitchen of the cottage. Sometimes it is night, sometimes it is daylight but, always, when I answer the phone, Jarlath is on the other end. Sometimes he speaks and sometimes he doesn't but I never have any doubt as to who is calling.

When he does speak, it's about things that are going on in my life in the nineties: about the end of my first marriage; about getting a mortgage for a house; about the children; about my state of mind. I find this last one most perplexing because, as far as I'm concerned, my state of mind is fine. In my head, it's late summer, early autumn 2005 and my head is clear and I'm dealing well with his death. Even within the dreams, I'm aware that the time and place of these conversations is wrong and out of kilter. Yes, within the dreams, I'm still living in Mullaghcreelan and, yes, I'm looking for a house I can afford to buy and, yes, the children are small but I'm also conscious that I've somehow moved on and that the now of 1992 is actually the then of thirteen years later.

But sometimes there is no voice from the other end of the telephone line – just the sound of his breathing. I ask if he's ok. I ask if there is anything I can do but nothing comes back. I just sit and listen to the sound of his inhalation and exhalation, coming in short even waves, unlike his stressed gasps that marked our last day together.

I read some articles about phone calls and what they can mean in dreams but there are no major insights – they suggest the same things I've been thinking: that the dreams symbolise a reaching out from somebody beyond contact; that they suggest an emotional sundering that can't or hasn't been bridged; some suggest the calls are a communication from another realm. Another article suggests the phone calls mean I'm trying to distance myself from a situation, but I want and need information about that situation. Yet another suggests it's a sign that the person on the other end of the line is doing well, getting on with things, happy even. And yet another suggests such dreams are a sign of repressed feelings. You pays your money and you takes your chances, I think, and then I stop reading the articles altogether.

Brother Ghost

You were a firm believer. You loved the liturgy and the long-established music of the Catholic Church. You missed the Latin Mass in which we'd both been grounded as altar boys.

You served Mass for Canon Cotter in the days when everything was in Latin and the priest celebrated Mass with his back to the congregation.

I began my altar career in the Latin days and made the crossover into English after Vatican II. You had a fondness for breaking into Latin, running passages from the Mass at will. Out of the blue, you'd perform the old routine: *In nominee Patris, et Fílii, et Spíritus Sancti. Amen. Introíbo ad altáre Dei qui laetificat juventútem meam*. Or it might be a well-sung verse of the "Tantum Ergo:"

Tantum ergo Sacramentum
Veneremur cernui;
Et antiquum documentum
Novo cedat ritui:
Praestet fides supplementum
Sensuum defectui.

Your career as an altar boy was a bit more successful than mine but we each carried the thurible with its gentle swing; inhaled the perfume of the incense; had a respect for the paten and a fascination with the Latin language throughout our lives.

Son

Truths are no longer true. The man in the mirror looks back at me, this ageing man whose appearance sometimes frightens me.

I never became the man I thought I would become. I never managed to be the man others needed. How often have I lain beside someone, knowing they were lonely, and been unable to reach them emotionally?

I've been there to walk and chat, with ease, on a May or October evening, but rarely been able to maintain those moments of connection.

A regression therapist once told me my inability to connect stems from the loss of my twin in the womb. I have no idea of the veracity of that judgment.

Father

When he was a young boy of twelve, Jarlath cycled the fourteen-mile round trip, to and from Carlow, to secondary school. He was a small boy on a big bicycle, wind and rain; twilight and dusk; September to June. That would have been our mother's idea but our father was fully behind her. Get a good education. Education was everything, the teacher in her said.

And our father would have agreed: 'Your mother is right, get a good education.' Whenever we under-achieved or whenever it looked like we might not be committed to our education he would come up with the same phrase, a warning to Jarlath or myself: 'If you're not careful you'll end up shovelling coal in Cope's yard.'

When Dolores was born someone remarked on how she looked like one or other of her aunts. Jack was clear in his response.

'I don't care who she looks like once she has her mother's brains.'

Our parents would have pushed Jarlath to go on with his education; there was no question of not doing it, no choice. That was 1954. We were still living on the Low Terrace, still four years away from moving to the High Terrace with its bathroom and its sitting-room and its three upstairs bedrooms. So every morning he and a few other boys and girls would head up Barn Hill on their bikes, the long push out of the village, then downhill past Wright's farm and on through Knocknagee and into Carlow to school. I knew nothing about this. I was the bow-legged two-year old on the swing, falling when I walked, walking when I could.

Just as I knew nothing of my father's twenty-mile round trips by bike, to and from work in Athy – winter and summer, day and night.

For Jarlath, not only was there the daily grind of cycling to and from school but there were piano lessons thrown in on Saturday afternoons, when he'd finished his half-day of schooling. He got the better of our mother on that one, though. Spent the time in the cinema or with his friends, spent the money for the lessons, did his piano practice in the evenings but never went to class. I admired his coolness in carrying that off. I couldn't have, but, by the time I got to hear the story, the storm had blown over and it was just another laughable legend, a story our father would tell at Christmas: *Do you remember the time....* It was a story he loved to tell.

Son

I make a deal with God. It's a month since Jarlath's Irish funeral and I've long been struggling to find any faith. Whenever I'm pushed, I describe myself as an agnostic Quaker. But in those weeks after the burial I sit down and talk to the God whose existence I doubt – and if S/He does exist, I've no doubt S/He is impressed by the fact that I'm willing to leave the door open. Very big of me!

I know I want to believe and I decide I'm going to try to believe for a year. I'm going to approach everything with an open mind but also with a willingness to trust in the hereafter. Even in my darkest days, I have never stopped praying. For me, prayer has always been a way of requesting, pleading, bargaining and hoping. Even when I stopped believing I went on praying. I abandoned the Hail Mary and Gloria of my childhood but I stuck with the Lord's Prayer because it has such a powerful, beautiful and wonderful aspiration. The idea that somehow the people of the world will be given their daily spiritual, emotional and bodily sustenance; the thought that our transgressions will be forgiven and that each of us might be given the strength to forgive in turn; the possibility that we will be resilient enough to avoid temptation and the prospect of being delivered from evil can't but be a celebration of the hopes and the desires of that entity we call soul.

When I pray now, I treat prayer as a way of thinking about and remembering people. I begin with the living, those I love and those I have known well. I think about them and what they meant and mean to me, how they brought or bring joy into my life. Then I think about the scattered friends and family who have died. I remember a moment of meeting, a time of celebration, an instant of joy. I try to picture them in those times and places. Finally, I do a virtual tour of the cemetery at Coltstown. I start at the grave of my stepmother, Debbie; cross to the burial places of Margaret Behan and

John and Pat Clowry; move on to the grave of our next door neighbours, Lil and Micheál Hunt; then over the low wall to the resting place of Liam Dunne, my school friend and one of the kindest, gentlest people I ever knew, who died when he was nine; then up the path to Peter Murphy, the man who ran the village cinema for years and brought light into our lives; from there I move to our neighbours from the Low Terrace, Jim and Mary Whelan and Vera and Jack Hickey and Dinah and Tim Whelan and the O'Rourkes and Byrnes and Farrells, and then on between the headstones to the resting places of our neighbours from the High Terrace, Bride and Tom O'Connell. I picture them sitting on the metal bench in their open porch, the evening sun setting in their eyes, their perfect gardens – front and back, flower and vegetable – immaculate in the fading light. Next door to them in the cemetery are my parents, Una and Jack. I remember the afternoon they and the O'Connells drove together to this place, to meet the caretaker and choose these adjacent plots – neighbours in life and death.

I picture my parents, again on a summer evening, working away in the front garden. Today, my father is trimming the edges of the lawn, my mother is watering the flowers, a bucket of water by her side, a cup in her hand, each flower getting its meticulously measured drink. There is peace, there are warm words and there is laughter.

I think of my brother and, often, I remember my college friend, Roberta. I imagine them walking together in the evening sunlight, chatting, finding common ground, one as cynical and funny as the other.

Why do I do that? Why do I never want to imagine Jarlath alone on the paths between the graves? There are other people of his generation buried in

Coltstown, school companions, neighbours, acquaintances but, in some way, *I* need him not to be alone, I want him to be entertained, amused, challenged, happy. That's my prayer now – that all these souls, remembered as people, have found a peace and a steadiness that eluded them in the days of their lives.

So, for that year, from the autumn of 2005 through to the end of 2006, I try to be a believer. I try to have the faith that my brother had. I do it in the hope that something of his conviction will rub off on me. And I do it in the hope that faith will bring certainty, the certainty of seeing him again; of being with him at some future time; of knowing that the unfinished conversations will be completed; of sensing the touch of his hand on my shoulder; of seeing the light in his eyes; of sharing the laughter of brothers. I open myself to these possibilities, to these hopes and wants and wishes.

One Sunday, during Quaker Meeting, I stumble across Minnie Louise Haskins' poem, "The Gate of the Year":

And I said to the man who stood at the gate of the year:
'Give me a light that I may tread safely into the unknown.'
And he replied:
'Go out into the darkness and put your hand into the Hand of God.
That shall be to you better than light and safer than a known way.'
So I went forth, and finding the Hand of God, trod gladly into the night.
And He led me towards the hills and the breaking of day in the lone East.

I want to move towards the hills and the breaking day because I have, in that time, a tendency towards hope and a faith that my brother might just be there waiting for me, as he's always been in life.

Brother Ghost

After your death, I was lost. Nothing looked or sounded the same any more. Of course, a part of that uncertainty was fear. Fear of the disease. Fear of death. Fear of being next in line. Fear of what might be around the corner. What might be in the blood. Fear of what might be in the brain.

I went, willingly and unwillingly, to the darkest places I could find. Places from which there seemed no escape. I longed for a warm, slow stroll with you, another ramble across that evening beach below the balcony of your summer home; I longed for one last, late-night conversation that travelled backward and forward, its breaks filled with quiet laughter – conscious not to disturb the sleepers above our heads.

I tried to dream good dreams of you but those dreams refused to run. I wore your old sweat shirt, the one emblazoned with *Duke*. I went to the place where your ashes lie and I listened but no one spoke. I doubted everything but most of all I doubted me, my life, my sanity. I woke up suspecting the truth. I went on with what we call living, day to day. I went to work and did my job. I laughed sometimes and then resented my own laughter. I tried to pray but my prayers were newspaper pages in the wind. I drove past the old house and stared at the empty window of the room that had been ours. I tried to understand what was happening. I decorated the Christmas tree. I lost my mind but, to be honest, the loss was not so great.

I wanted to believe the things that you'd believed. I wanted your faith, your hope, your great trust in the things that we'd been taught. I wanted you to be, just that, simply to have you here. I walked each day as though I were walking through hedges of holly. I was fearful and then I was afraid of that fear. I wanted never to forget any moment that had you in it. I longed for forgetfulness. I kept your email address on my computer and it's still there. I kept your phone number in my book. I framed your photograph and photographs of the pair of us together. I bought some Mozart CDs. I played the music that you knew and loved. I walked and walked, as though you might somehow be waiting in the forest. I watched my dog for signs of some sixth sense. I lost the bearings of that place that divides want from need. I cried. I was afraid of how we grow to be the very thing we fear.

Son

It's the October after my brother's death and I've started hearing things, not voices in my head, not the voices of the dead but I've definitely started hearing things. Mostly it has to do with music. Often, when I'm driving and the radio is on, the music being played sounds odd. Well-known songs that I grew up with sound out of tune.

I listen and I can't believe they're so off key. What I'm hearing is dissonance rather than harmony. This happens only when I'm driving and only when I'm alone. It's an eerie feeling, as though something that's been taken for granted all my life is suddenly exposed as something completely different and unrecognisable.

The first time it happens is on the motorway. Willie Nelson is singing "Stardust." The serene voice is crooning about each kiss being an inspiration. Then he reaches the line about the garden wall and everything is out of tune, unfocused. Something is radically wrong. But then the song hits the guitar riff and, when the voice reappears, everything is back on track and the voice is again in tune.

Sometimes there are days and sometimes weeks between these episodes.

And then it's November, an afternoon early in the month, one of those days when I know that every last trace of summer is truly gone. The air is cold and wet and there's an urgent threat of winter waiting on the corner, its coat pulled tight about its throat, hat drawn low across its eyes, promising only bitter rain.

I'm in the kitchen, preparing some food for the evening meal. I'm alone. I walk from the kitchen, through the dining room. The dog is sleeping under the table and I stop to throw some logs in the stove and, as I do, he opens one eye, rolls onto his back and stretches lazily, before dozing off again. All these details are embossed on my mind, as though something in my brain has already sensed the importance of these last few moments of sanity. I step into the hall at the foot of the stairs and turn on the light. Tired of listening to politicians on the radio, I want to get some music from my study. I want something low and slow, something with lyrics I can bathe in, not just listen to but travel through and travel with, something filled with the kiss and snarl that marks the human condition with its soft or bitter bruises.

The light from the hallway has dribbled down the corridor to my study door, diluting the late afternoon dullness and, as I turn, I catch sight of it from the corner of my eye, scampering along the corridor to my right, bigger than a rat and blacker but scurrying as rats and mice do, keeping close to the skirting board, along the length of two rooms. When it gets to the study door it turns and scuttles to the opposite wall, disappearing behind a radiator. I freeze, my fear of rats rising like a sickness through my belly and throat. The impulse is there to run but there's another, stronger impulse that has always made me go in search of some way to deal with the things that terrify me.

I remember a day in a different house when I had climbed up to the attic to lay poison for mice and came face to face with two rats on a rafter. The urge to run away had been there then, too, but I'd stayed in the house, checked the poison day by day and, eventually, smelled the strangely satisfying sweetness of their decaying bodies.

The dread of fear has always been the thing that frightens me most. My immediate response is to wade in and face whatever it is that needs facing, deal with it while the adrenalin is flowing. And that's what I do on that November afternoon in 2005. I walk quickly down the corridor, determined to do whatever needs doing. I will sort this out and that will be that.

The corridor is empty. There's nothing behind the radiator, there are no holes in the floorboards, no scrapings or scratches on the wall plaster and nowhere else the creature could have gone but back the way it had come. What do I feel? Is it relief? Not in the least. Instead I feel the terror intensify inside me, the fist stiffen in my stomach, the nausea thicken in my throat. And then I see it again, this time in the hallway, racing along the wooden floor, noiseless but with the same darting run. It crosses the rug outside the kitchen door and disappears under the stairs. I take a torch from the desk in my study and go to find it in the darkness beneath the steps but, when I look, it isn't there. Obviously, I tell myself, it has run elsewhere while I was collecting the torch. The question is, where has it gone? Has it scuttled into the dining room or the kitchen? Is it skulking in the narrow space behind the dishwasher? Or has it found the gap in the kitchen floorboards and made its way into the darkness beneath them? If that's the case it could be anywhere, already working its way inside the studded walls, climbing and scurrying. I may hear it presently, snouting about in the bedrooms upstairs.

And then a wind outside lifts the dried and fallen leaves from the garden, scattering them across the glass panels of the double door. They rise and plummet, grazing the glass as they fall, a sound like tiny nails scuttering on timber, a sound like a dark rat racing, a sound that petrifies me.

I don't see the scurrying form again that afternoon, nor do I hear it that night and by the end of the week I have more or less forgotten it. But the following week it reappears, in the corridor, racing along beside the skirting board, this time disappearing through the open doorway into my study. And so the pattern is established. The hallway, the stairs, the corridor – always and only in those places, always caught out of the corner of my eye, always petrifying, always pummelling into my stomach, forcing the bile into my throat, leaving me constantly on edge, waiting for the next appearance and the next.

It's not until early December that I begin to realise what this creature really is but that doesn't lessen the terror. It doesn't stop the sense of apprehension in my gut as I open the front door in the evening. It doesn't ease the fear with which I step into the twilit hallway or turn to face the corridor. It doesn't stop me listening for the sound of something I can never absolutely know, even when I recognise it for the thing it is – my sadness made flesh.

Father

It's been so many years and I've never spoken or written about this. It's like a reason I can't find or an excuse I can't offer. Yet every time I pass the hospital in Athy I think of it and, just today, while I was driving, I heard a song called "Ghost in my car" and I knew I had to write the story down because there is a ghost in my car and always will be.

It was 1998 and the doctor had recommended – more than recommended, he had, to use his own words, 'very seriously urged' – that my father should spend some time in the local hospital. It was a question of his need for medical care, the doctor said, a question of respite. It was, as we'd expected, a suggestion that my father had resisted for a long, long time.

'It's for two weeks, just two weeks,' I told him.

He nodded but was silent. The clock ticked. The fire burned and spat.

'Two weeks has a way of becoming an awful lot longer,' he said at last.

'I know that but, believe me; this is just for two weeks.'

The matter was put aside, to be revisited whenever and, of course whenever might be never.

But my father's condition worsened.

'He really does need around-the-clock nursing at the moment,' the doctor said. 'It's not just advisable, it's imperative.'

The subject was broached again, this time by the doctor. His mixture of charm and persistence, and a promise that my father would, definitely, be home in a few weeks eventually swayed the argument and a date was set.

It was my responsibility to take my father to the hospital. Arriving at his house that lunchtime, I found him waiting, his overcoat wrapped, two sizes too big, around him.

'Available but not enthusiastic,' as he said himself.

And so we set off, on the familiar ten-mile journey. The journey I estimated he had made twenty thousand times in a working life, twice a day; the journey that I had taken with him in my primary school years; the journey we had made winter and summer in the Morris Minor and, later, the Austin A40. Out past Mullaghcreelan Hill, down into Kilkea village; through Grangenolvin and Bray and into Athy; over the railway bridge and past the railway station, where he had worked for most of his adult life. The great silence remained unbroken as we edged through the mid-afternoon traffic.

Over the Barrow Bridge and right, onto the Stradbally Road, finally turning through the hospital gates, the imposing edifice, built in the Famine years, looming against the blue of the sky. Only then did my father speak. 'I never thought you'd put me in the County Home.'

To my father, this building would always be the County Home and the sight of its soaring, grey walls had brought almost ninety years of memory, suspicion and dread pouring out in that one sentence. To my father this was still the workhouse; the place where the unwanted, unrecognised, unkempt and undesired were dumped. It didn't matter that St Vincent's Hospital was and is a warm place, with an extraordinarily welcoming staff; it didn't matter that the facilities are modern; that he would be well nursed and well cared for or that he'd be coming home in a few weeks. He was a proud man and the stigma of the County Home, instilled in childhood, was still fresh, still raw, still humiliating.

He did come home that spring but the following autumn, as the bushes berried in the ditches, his doctor recommended another stint in the hospital. I didn't have the heart or soul – what am I saying? – I didn't have the courage to drive him there on that occasion. Instead, I accepted my cousin, Peter's, kind offer to be his chauffeur.

When I went to visit my father, he was in a ward with two other CIE men – two hundred and fifty years of living and one hundred and forty-one years of railway service between them, three old steam engines parked in a final siding. And this time there was no going home. My father died in that hospital the following spring, two weeks short of his ninety-first birthday.

And some days his ghost travels with me in the car and some days we laugh – but some days he reminds me about that journey all those years ago and I still shiver at the thought.

Son

It's the summer of 2009 and I know I have to begin this book. Foolishly, I believe I can finish it in six months. All the stories are there, the emotion is there, the memories are there and something keeps tapping on my shoulder, telling me I owe it to Jarlath and to myself to get the story told.

Is that urge driven by the fact that my second marriage is following my first onto the rocks, that I have become impossible to live with, that running away from a relationship yet again seems the only thing to do? I tell myself that a month away from home, a month by the sea, a month of writing will clear my head of the spectres and manifestations that have been haunting me for more than three years. And I believe, or I tell myself I believe, that the time away will give everyone the opportunity to step back from the awful sadness I have brought into the house and can't dispel.

So off I set. Travelling light, bringing only the essentials. A couple of books of poetry; one bag of clothes, a notebook and my laptop. I go for all kinds of reasons but I tell myself that, like Thoreau:

I went ... because I wished to live deliberately, to front only the essential facts of life, and see if I could not learn what it had to teach, and not, when I came to die, discover that I had not lived. I did not wish to live what was not life, living is so dear; nor did I wish to practise resignation, unless it was quite necessary. I wanted to live deep and suck out all the marrow of life, to live so sturdily and Spartan-like as to put to rout all that was not life, to cut a broad swath and shave close, to drive life into a corner, and reduce it to its lowest terms, and, if it proved to be mean, why then to get the whole and genuine meanness of it, and publish its meanness to the world; or if it were sublime, to know it by experience, and be able to give a true account of it in my next excursion.

But, of course, when I fool myself into believing I can go and be someone new, shaking off the lethargy and unhappiness that have plagued me all my life and, more particularly, in the years, since my brother's death, I find that I carry that very sadness and inertia and frustration with me and that, once I'm alone in a beautiful house by the sea, the darkness multiplies and breeds.

I've brought no music with me. I want to be clear of every outside influence, I tell myself. But there is music in the house. No television but a handful of CDs. One of them is a compilation, a give-away with some Sunday newspaper. One of the tracks on it is Crystal Gayle singing "Crying in the Rain." It becomes a kind of anthem and I listen to it over and over. *You'll never know that I still love you so, though the heartaches remain.* I have no idea why I'm even listening to a song I've heard a thousand times but some days the heartaches are for my brother, some days for my wife, some days for me and every day for the complete mess I've made of my life. That hackneyed song seems to say everything I want to say or need someone to say to me.

I know the preceding six months have been a nightmare for Caitriona. The previous January I'd told her I wanted to get out of our marriage. The day I first mentioned that possibility had been a grey day and by evening the skies had unloaded a couple of hours of snow. For five days we were more or less snowed in, stuck in the same house. Then one morning, with the countryside buried under a sky-fallen avalanche, we made a break for it and spent hours walking the snowbound lanes that bordered the bog close to where we lived. We talked and talked and talked. A few weeks later, we went and talked to a counsellor and through that spring it seemed as if there might be something to be saved but, in the end, whatever was there wasn't enough.

One of us says how much easier life would be if couples reached the same points of falling in and out of love at the same time but that's not how life is – the cup shatters in different ways at different times and the pieces never quite seem to fit together again afterwards; a shard is missing here, a corner there, and the smoothness is gone for ever. The cracks keep on reminding that what was is gone, and what you hoped for in a life is never going to be that way again, because there is no going back.

And so, all these months later, I find myself doing the running, putting this book forward as the reason – or excuse – for getting away.

The house I rent is bright and airy, with an enormous garden and views across the sea. The beach is just a fifteen-minute walk away – long and wide and mostly deserted. I am ahead of the tourist rush, the schools not yet out, the lanes and country roads are mostly my own and the weather smiles on me.

I have a daily routine of getting up early; eating; walking; trying to write; walking again after lunch and then trying, again, to write. The sentences are put down and are deleted at the end of each afternoon. Either I don't have anything to say or I can't say it.

Each night I walk the beach for an hour and tell myself I need a good kick – that I should be writing, I should be happy with the very good life I have, I should be tending to my garden, I should be counting the lucky stars shining on my living. But the invisible, burning, black haze, the dog-shadow that follows me from time to time is sitting pretty at my feet by then and nothing will shift it and nothing will come when I take a seat before the empty page.

I cannot write. In my four weeks in that house, I produce one solitary paragraph. The words won't come; they're backed up behind the more recent sadnesses and failures of a relationship fallen apart, behind that sense of my having fucked up *again.*

As the weeks pass and the haze thickens, I reach a point where it seems as if nothing will ever be right. I can't get over my brother's death; I can't make a success of a marriage; I can't write and I can't see where my life is going. Work, friendships, family, possibilities all seem to be evaporating at the same time and it isn't as if circumstances or anyone else is to blame. I am surrounded by people who love me and care for me, people who are willing to put their own lives and love on the line for me, to support me in every way they can. And yet I can't reciprocate those feelings and that concern. Nothing is possible, nothing is working; my energy has gone and all that's left is the ruin of so many lives and so many aspirations. No one else is to blame for anything that has happened to me and there are no excuses for the coldness with which I surrounded myself in the previous months. It's the coldness of death.

One night, in the third week of my time away, I drive to a lighthouse a dozen miles from where I'm staying. I park the car and walk across a field and out onto the rocks above the sea. To my right is the rising white mass of the nineteenth-century building, its lamp still unlit. To my left are the rocks that spread in jagged mathematics out into the waves. I walk to the left. The rocks rise in layers, a natural amphitheatre. I climb to the Gods and look down into the moving sea that clambers between those rocks on which I'm standing and the stone that forms the other side of the inlet. There's a drop of thirty feet into the white ridges of the incoming waves and then a drop into the darker, denser water that remains as the waves are sucked back out into the open sea.

I realise that I've driven here this evening not with an intention but with a possibility in my head. I had spent the morning trying, again unsuccessfully, to write and the afternoon walking the lanes that wound around the house. My brain was incapable of getting beyond the litany of failure that seemed to sum up my life. Yes, I'd held jobs, made a living, published a handful of books, made some radio programmes, even won a couple of accolades along the way but, in truth, what I had left in my wake – and that word was uppermost in my mind – was a failed marriage, a failing marriage and a sense that nothing I had done would ever amount to anything more than letting people down. These were the people who had supported me, loved me, stood by me and put up with me for years and yet, in the end, I couldn't stay in any one place. It seemed, on that sunny evening, that this not only had been but would be the sum of my life. To fail once, I told myself, was understandable, to fail twice was selfishness. I loathed what I'd become, and I detested who I was and what I'd done. I saw no point in my life and not alone had I no expectation but I couldn't even countenance the possibility that I might receive forgiveness or, indeed, deserve it.

And so I find myself above the pounding, sucking surge of the sea and I think about how easy it would be to take one step forward, out over the clean, clear fall of the rocks, nothing between me and the deep, dark water but choice. The easiest way to go, I've heard people say speculatively. A feeling of calm and contentment, like falling asleep, I've read. Once the first shock is over, once the struggle and doubts have ended there is nothing but peace and a feeling of well-being. Everything over. No one particularly distraught. Finances organised. The end of a troubled line where the train runs gently into the sea and disappears for ever, not even a solitary puff of smoke left as a reminder.

But, instead, cowardice or resolve take me back across the rocks, to the base of the lighthouse and there I sit until darkness eases its way across the sky and the light above me begins its intermittent flashing, its beam slashing out across the waves, here and gone, here and gone. And I think of the buoys off the Carolina coast, their death knells ringing and their metal bodies rolling in the sea. And then I drive back to my rented house and sit late into the night.

I come back from my month in the country, come home with nothing written and little resolved.

It's a summer evening as I park the car outside our house, the day still warm, the sun still high above the orchard and wood we'd set a decade earlier, the trees grown tall and broad, marking the years we've spent together. We'd had plans for that small wood, plans to build a cabin there – a retreat from the world, a place for Caitriona to draw, for me to write. A place to sleep on summer nights, a space to watch the falling snow climb down between the trees, stepping from branch to branch, before resting on the earth.

The only thing I know on this summer evening is that I am about to run again, to step, again, out of a marriage in search of something else. That is the information I've brought home with me, for as long as this house remains *home*. I want Caitriona to be as unsettled, as uncommitted as I am. But what I find is a warm welcome; beautifully cooked food; flowers on the table; the house and garden filled with the touches that make it home.

And when I go to leave my unused notebook in my study I find Caitriona has repainted the floor. The room is suddenly bright and airy, the windows open, the warm breeze blowing through. There are flowers on my desk, the mess I left has been tidied, everything is in its place. The fire is already set in the stove, ready for the first blasts of autumn and winter, still months away.

I sit at that desk, the smell of flowers and the warm air from the garden swaddling me and I know the kindness, the consideration, the love and the care will never be enough because nothing, it seems, will ever be enough to keep me in one place, one state of mind, one time of contentment. My life with Caitriona has been filled with thoughtfulness; she has loved me, has been kindness itself; I have received a far greater love than I expected or deserved, and yet it has not been enough to make me appreciate the gifts I've been given.

I sit there and look around the tidied room; stand on the recently painted floor; sit at the desk with its order and neatness and know there is nothing to do but to leave, to disrupt lives, to walk, to run, to disappear – just as I'd done before.

That night, long after Caitriona has gone to bed, long after the sadness I have carried back with me has settled on the house – as it so often does – like a squat cat smothering a small baby, I sit again at the neatly ordered desk and listen to Jacques Brel singing "The Desperate Ones" and know exactly what he is saying. I recognise the people whose lives he recorded. The haunted figures, struggling hand in hand, down empty streets, their shadows like silent companions beside them. I see them walking into the setting sun and I know that feeling of pulling that same sun from the sky, leaving the ones who love me, the ones I love in my own bleak and crooked way, in darkness. I think of the desperate ones disappearing from the bridge of nevermore – across it or off it, we're never sure until the song moves on. And I remember that night at the lighthouse and I wonder, again, if it would have been a kinder and a braver thing to have ended it there and then. But a song is a song. The lyrics, the music generate a mood; generate a moment for contemplation; create a picture; bring characters to life. Real life, however, and the cruelties we impose on other people don't end in four minutes; they blow like bloodied bandages across the fields and gardens and rooms of our lives, leaving gore and heart-breaking reminders in the wake of their passing.

We're sitting at the small, round table in the consultation room, the completed paperwork lies between us.

‘You know,’ the solicitor smiles, ‘we’ve done a lot of divorce work in this office, over the years, but you’re the first person who has come to us for a second divorce. The next one is free.’

And then we talk about something else.

Afterwards, driving the winding road between his office and home, stuck behind three crawling drivers who seem to have escaped from a summer Sunday afternoon, a surge of remorse and failure washes over me and I think of waves.

To my right, across the low and scrappy winter ditch, the land from Levitstown Mill to Maganey is flooded. The Barrow has burst its banks again, swallowing the coarse fields and scrubby bushes that litter this often desolate landscape. Even in summer, the low ground gives off an air of marshy desolation. It’s a landscape for passing through, not a place I’d want to live. So, maybe it’s the swampy countryside, overrun with dark choppy water that brings back the thoughts of the waves. Whatever the reason, they come.

At first the waves are the low, slow rollers of Carolina beaches, warm Atlantic breakers that reflect the blueness of the sky and the light of the sun and the heat of the day. But it’s impossible to keep that memory alive on a road that has this sluggish, cold deluge on its shoulder. Even with the car heater running, the chill seeps through me and I’m standing on another shoreline while the high, hard waves of the Celtic Sea batter the early summer rocks around that lighthouse.

And, on this winter afternoon, with the swollen river already settling in the dykes beside the road and the three crawling cars still meandering along the twisted way, my suitcase feels as if it will never again be lifted from the back seat of this car. I am moving, once more.

I know it's filled, not with stones but with all these photographs of happier days, so many sad reminders of all the occasions I helped create with such passion; the great ideas and the celebrations and remembrances that enthused me; the plans and preparations for big days and small: the dinner guests; the laughter; the poetry of friendship and the tedious prose of losing friendship; the lengthy, slow nights of teasing out the great and stimulating questions of our lives. But in the end, and inevitably, there followed the mad, mysterious destruction I brought upon the heads of those I tried to love.

I laugh, this time in the silence of the car, its tyres turning wetly on the damp, slow road. I'm laughing at the emptiness I feel and I'm laughing at the futility of this dry, hard laughter that is nothing but a mockery of joy.

Brother Ghost

On bad days, it seems to me that your life came down to this: a Dunlop Warwick tennis ball box with bits and pieces stored inside. A pair of silver Blue Devil cuff links you gave me. I've never worn cuff links but I've kept these because...well, you never know. A letter to you, dated 4 November 1963 – just weeks before the death of JFK – from the Academic Council in UCD, reminding you, as editor of the student paper *Awake*, that "the continuation of the permission given to you to sell in the College depends upon your not carrying advertisements for dances which are run outside the College without College approval or sanction." Inside the envelope are two newspaper clippings from the time, reporting on your stand against the Academic Council. And there are envelopes of stamps, addressed to *Master Jarlath MacKenna, Redemptorist College, Limerick*. And yet another letter, dated 28 August 1963, from Father McKinley, headmaster of the Redemptorist College. It's addressed to you at your digs in Lynton Road in Acton, London, where you were working for the summer. It made for interesting reading. You'd obviously spoken to him about your hopes, having taken your B.A. and H. Dip. from UCD, of going on to study medicine.

My Dear Jarlath,

With your permission, I am writing to your mother, by this post, to learn whatever I can about your parents' position and their plans for the future. I know that they will not stand in your way should you decide to take up medicine – but I know, too, that you would not wish them to let you enter on a course that was going to involve them in great sacrifice. However, I hope you will be patient with me; it may be another fortnight before I can find time to write to you. The boys return on Monday and I don't suppose I will have much time for letter-writing during the first two weeks of new term.

Did you ever think of spending a few years on the foreign missions, as a teacher? At the moment we are looking for a secondary teacher who would spend three years in our "Ginasio" – our secondary school in Pedro Afonso, Brazil. Already we have three Irish lads working with us – one an Agricultural Inspector, the second – his brother – a Technical Teacher (Building Construction) and the third, a mechanic. I don't expect you would be interested since it would interfere with your plans for beginning the study of medicine and the salary would not be more that £30 a month. However, I felt I should mention it, since I know you would be eager to play an active part in the Apostolate, if the opportunity offered. You had such an ambition at one time, I'm sure it's not dead. Please do not misunderstand me. I do not wish to suggest that you <u>*should*</u> *undertake this work. There are other forms of the apostolate in which you could play a worthy part; many opportunities will offer themselves if you do qualify in medicine. But, knowing your innate goodness, I just wanted to inform you of this opening, in case you would wish to avail of it. I know that whatever role you fill in life, you will always try to play a full part in bringing others to the love of God. Pray!*

Best wishes, Jarlath – and again, kind regards to John. I look forward to meeting you in October.

The financial pressure was obviously on at home; you were calling in the troops to give you backing and the troops – or at least this one – was suggesting that you spend some time thinking about your decision and working on the missions.

No doubt, our mother would have been impressed by any letter from the headmaster in the Redemptorist College. Oh, and I noticed he had his eye on me as a potential sub for you in the clerical stakes, given that he had lost you! Were you happy, in your digs in Acton, with what he said? Did you feel he'd row in behind you?

Years later, long after you'd qualified, you went to New Mexico and spent a time working there with Native Americans. Clare told me it was an eye-opener, given the poor medical services but that you'd really enjoyed the experience. 'It was challenging,' she said, 'but, as usual, he rose to it.' Again, always again, I wish we'd talked some more about it.

And there was your social insurance card, also from 1963, stamped for the weeks you worked, including the two weeks up to Christmas – Post Office work. And a postcard congratulating you on getting your H. Dip. – from *Tom, Dick & Harry*. It was postmarked Galway and had a photograph of Salthill. And another card from David in Bavaria, telling you about how he and his friends have been watching the Fräuleins and that *bikinis are a dime a dozen and the birds are ok* and *the language barrier is surmountable*. Apart from that, and a scatter of a couple of dozen stamps, the only other thing in the box was a smaller cardboard box containing a rolled up contact sheet of photographs from around the time of your graduation.

There we all were in the tiny pictures of the period: the five of us, our mother in a purple coat, our father in a suit, Dolores in a grey costume and me in my short-trousered suit – the last suit I ever owned. And there you were on your own, parchment in hand. You with Clare. You with one of our cousins, Declan Bray. And a photograph of our mother in a hospital bed, after she'd collapsed at your graduation. And that was it – part of the story of a year that changed your life. The same year I'd been shipped off for three months to Tír an Fhiadh, in the Connemara Gaeltacht, to improve my Irish.

Son

Sometime in the mid-1990s I made a series of documentaries for RTE Radio 1 on regression therapy. The series, researched by Derek Mooney, was called

"Going Back" and over the three programmes I went through various regressions. During one of those sessions the return was to the womb and afterwards the therapist talked to me about being a twin and losing my fellow twin before birth. At the time, it was something I found interesting but not an idea I dwelled on for too long.

In more recent months I've found myself wondering about her theory and considering the possibility that my feeling of – or need for – exclusion; my craving to keep running from people and places during my life; my constant pursuit of a happier existence and a place of contentment stems from some innate sense of loss that I may have carried into the world; a feeling of fragmentation that spiralled so often into fruitless searching for answers to questions I hadn't even formulated.

Father

Once, when I was a young boy, my father and I were about to get into the car. It had been parked in the shelter of a cherry blossom at Athy railway station, my father's workplace. As he unlocked the door a breeze lifted the branches of the tree and a shower of cerise and white blossoms rose and then fell quietly across our shoulders.

'Isn't that just beautiful?' my father said.

Decades later, as I was running on a river bank, the May blossoms cut loose above me, their petals cascading as I ran, the dandelion clocks ticking beneath my feet. And I thought about the fall of the cherry on that day so long ago and the fall of the May and how I have always been running,

running for my life. And I thought of my father and how, like each of us, his last breath had been expelled between the falling of one burst of blossom and the next. His eyes closing on the world at last and fully and how, in time, I too will fall as the May and cherry flowers fell.

Brother Ghost

The dreams returned, seven years after you'd died. And when they came, they came in layers but always with that old common thread woven through them, dreams of my being somewhere and you being nearby, in sight but silent. Then they stopped for a couple of months but they came again, at Christmas. Only this time there were other people in them.

In one dream I was standing on a street in Naas, waiting for the Dublin bus. It was a wet evening and when the bus stopped the driver signalled that it was full. Through the fogged glass I could see throngs of people I knew – a young girl who had been killed in a fall from a horse in her teens; an ex-girlfriend from college days; neighbours; lost friends, all of them dead. And you.

As the bus pulled away, I asked a young man standing beside me where the bus was going.

'That's the dead bus,' he said. 'It brings dead people home for the weekend.'

A week later there was another dream. This time, I found myself in a huge department store in Dublin. There were crowds of people shopping and it was late in the evening. But all of the other shoppers were dead people who were known to me. My parents were there and there were children running about the place, children whom I knew to be dead. And you were there.

'We have a special shopping night on the last Thursday before Christmas,' the woman at the perfume counter told me, 'just for people who are dead.'

I didn't ask why I was there and she didn't offer an explanation.

But in none of these dreams, or the many others I had during the following spring and summer, did you ever speak. You were there – just beyond reach, just beyond contact, visible but silent. And then the dreams stopped and I missed your sad and soundless visits.

Father

I have this recording of my father singing some of the songs he loved. I listen to it and I'm back with him in the Morris Minor, driving home from Athy on a spring evening. We're coming through Kilkea and the hedges are blizzarding May flowers onto the road. We drive slowly through the flying storm of petals, caught on the warm breeze. And suddenly my father bursts into song, his voice strong, unforced and clear.

Oh Genevieve, I'd give the world to live again the lovely past,
the rose of youth is dew impearled but now it withers in the blast.
I see thy face in all my dreams, my waking thoughts are full of thee,
thy glance is like the starry beam, that falls along the summer sea.
Oh Genevieve, sweet Genevieve, the days may come, the days may go,
but still the hand of memory weaves the blissful dreams of long ago.

Then he pulls the car to the side of the road and opens the window and the surge of Mayflower flitters and swirls around us and he laughs out loud and I laugh too. And when we get home, my mother looks at us, our hair and clothes doused in the confetti of the white, early summer and she says: 'Aren't ye the right pair of stooks!' but her eyes are shining and her mouth can't hide a smile and my father bursts into song again:

Only a pansy blossom, only a withered flower

yet to me it's far dearer than all in earth's fair bower.

And later still, as I cross the garden on my way to the football field, my father is still singing as he turns the soil on another potato drill.

Brother Ghost

I dream of you but you're not really in my dream, at least not at the heart of it. You're standing out there at the edge, here but not here, watching and waiting but not directly involved. It seems this will always be the way with you in my dreams. Just the way I imagine you now – here but not here, on the periphery of my life, of all our lives.

The dream begins on a mountain road, somewhere out on the north-west coast of the country, with the sea again and waves and cliffs that plunge like hardy swimmers into that sea. The sun is shining and the sky is clear but the water still has that menace that threatens to throw up the dead and the broken and surprise me with something – flesh, for instance, damaged to the point of repulsion. And above all this, on a slight incline, you stand watching two men on the narrow road. Your face and arms are cut and bruised, blood drying in the midday sun.

I ask why you don't come down to join me and you say something about the two men, that they forced you off the road, that they threatened you, that they beat you up. I look at you – standing way up there, beyond my reach – and then I look at the two men. They're in their late teens or early twenties. They don't speak and I don't ask them why they've done any of this. Instead, I walk towards them and, as I do, they begin to move towards me, sullen and silent. I lift a stick from the roadside, a sturdy branch, though there are no trees along this stretch of road. They're moving closer now and their faces are hard and sour, their heavy steps raise small clouds of dust from the dry ground. When they're ten feet from me, I can see the pale blue and clouded green of their eyes. One of them opens his mouth, as though he's about to speak but, before he has a chance to say anything, I raise the branch above my head and bring it smashing down on him. He crumples under the weight of the bough and, immediately, I swing it at his companion, catching him on the side of his face, ripping his skin and sending him to the ground, too. And, while they lie there, screaming, I go on beating and kicking them, silencing their voices, thrashing and pounding until they have no voices left, until their mouths are crooked gapes and their faces have the red rawness of uncooked meat, their blood beaten back into their flesh, until their skin loses all colour, until I know with certainty that they're dead. Only then do I pause to take stock of what I've done.

I turn and look back up the hillside, you're still standing there, still watching.

'You can come down now,' I say, but you make no attempt to move.

'It's done, they're dead,' I say. 'You can come back down.' But you shake your head, appalled, it seems to me, at what I've done.

I look back to the pair of crumpled bodies on the roadway and I realise the only thing connecting me to their deaths is the blood-spattered necktie I'm wearing. I look to you for guidance but you just go on staring. I'm on my own.

'I have to hide this tie,' I shout.

You say nothing. I feel the panic rising in me. It can't be long before someone arrives and finds me standing over the bodies.

'I have to burn this tie or get rid of it. I have to go.'

I wait for you to nod, to agree, to say something but still nothing comes, no response, no word of encouragement. Instead, you remain on the hill, staring down at me and the empty bodies on the sunlit road. I want to say, I've done all this for you. I want you to recognise that fact, to show sympathy but you don't and there's nothing I can do.

And then I'm off, in search of a place to hide the evidence. But wherever I go there's someone there before me. I can't dump the tie in the dustbin on the pier at the bottom of the hill because there are children playing there. I can't hide it in the empty house farther along the road because an elderly woman is picking flowers in the abandoned garden. I can't stuff it under the rocks at the water's edge because that part of the beach is full of holiday-makers. And, as in so many dreams, I have an innate knowledge. I know I'm being tracked by two policemen, dogged, heavy-set men. At first they're just specks in the distance but then I see them, still remote but determined, tramping the road behind me, stopping now and then to check for evidence. And there you stand, above the whole thing, watching, silent – always silent – a smudge on the backcloth of the hillside.

I wake and morning is about to break, the first light considering its few options and I'm relieved to be out of the dream and I miss you but I'm confused, too, by your refusal to help me, your look of disapproval at what I'd done. What I've done for you.

Father

It is February 1977. I walk into the quiet room in St Vincent's Hospital where my mother lies dying. My father is sitting by her bed, running his long fingers lightly through her thin hair, massaging her scalp. Her breathing goes on, sharp and low, her lungs drawing in the last moments of this life.

Brother Ghost

Years later, in the summer of 2022, my sister-in-law, Clare, will send me a letter you received from our mother. It was written a couple of weeks before her death. Her beautiful handwriting flows across the two pages of Basildon Bond paper, telling you about the awful weather; about the play I was directing; about my first slim volume of poetry which had just appeared. But it's the closing sentence that catches me unawares. *I'll write to Clare later - now Pop is waiting to post this.* In that one, brief sentence I am reminded of her term of endearment for our father and I catch a distant glimpse of a different kind of relationship, of a warmth and tenderness and love that was so rarely a part of the life I saw.

I see Una at the kitchen table, sealing and addressing the envelope; I see Jack waiting patiently, car keys in hand, to catch the last post; I imagine you doing your rounds in an American hospital, her letter on its way to you. I feel the sudden rush of cold as the back door is opened and Jack steps into the dark, icy January evening.

And I smile.

Son

Yesterday I turned seventy-one. Today a great darkness came – not in the shape of a crow, I love crows, love their impishness, their brashness, that *feck off* attitude in the way they refuse to move, in the tilt of their heads. It came in the shape of something else, dark and desperate and malign, and squatted on my shoulders; it got in behind my eyes and made it difficult for me to open them, it sucked the energy out of my body and left the world – despite the autumn sunshine and the golden, burning leaves which fell about me in Mullaghcreelan Wood – a dark and threatening place.

I'm now eight years older than my brother was when his life ran out. I am far beyond the days he lived, beyond the frontier he reached in life, in love and longing.

Brother Ghost

I have your stamp album here, battered and bruised but still intact. The album that you treasured, the way you cherished your Subbuteo set (which I broke because I was intrigued by how the men balanced on the buttons and the only way to have my unspoken questions answered was by taking one apart. When that failed to provide the answer, the only alternative was to take the next one apart and then the next) and your Meccano (which I damaged before I realised the pieces didn't bend in the way I expected and needed a little encouragement to form an arch under which my racing cars could pass) and your Dinky cars (which I regularly dismembered because the fitting of the tyres fascinated me). Cherished the way you cared for your Hornby train set, the one that was kept well out of my reach.

Dolores says I was a wild child, our Aunt Bridie described me as *a little devil* but I don't ever remember you saying a cross word to me. You must have done, you must have shown your frustration at my destructive streak, but I don't remember. Not that I set out to be destructive. It was just that I was captivated by the way things worked and my investigations inevitably led to their not working.

And it wasn't just your toys that caught my destructive attention. Later, when I was eleven or twelve, I'd build Airfix model planes; douse them in paraffin oil; set them alight and send them gliding out over the back garden from the roof of the shed, just so that I could visualise a plane crash.

Nor did it stop in childhood. There was that snagged tape of "Harper Valley PTA" and my teenage attempt to put it all together again.

But the stamp album has survived with its traces of faces and places. Did you dream of those faraway shores? Did you long to be in the countries whose stamps were brighter, bigger, brasher than our own sad, dark marks? Was there something – even then, even as a ten-year-old – that called you and promised you and drew you away from the monochrome of our little village?

Father

It's been years since I've dreamt of my parents and then, as I'm finishing this book, the dream comes. No great surprise there.

In the dream, I'm standing on the roadside in Coltstown, on the grass verge across the road from the cemetery where my parents' bodies and Jarlath's ashes are interred. It's evening, a warm summer evening. Only later in the dream do I realise it is July 2005.

My mother is sitting on the cemetery wall. She's a young woman, probably about the age she was when Jarlath was born. Her suntanned legs are dangling, she looks relaxed and happy, and she's reciting an old poem, one of the pieces that are neatly handwritten in her notebook, the one that sits in the drawer of my desk, beside my father's penknife:

The way is short, oh friend,
That reaches out before us.
God's tender heavens above us bend,
His love is smiling o'er us.
A little while is ours

For sorrow or for laughter,
I'll lay the hand you love in yours
On the shore of the Hereafter.

Her voice is quiet but she's speaking with the carefulness of someone who knows her recitation may be overheard by the sleepers in the ground behind her. One of the cherry trees that line the perimeter of the graveyard is spreading its dark, rich branches above her head and the sun is mottling her sunburnt face. The shadow of the tree falls hard across the bone dry ground, its tip lying at my feet.

I don't know how the news arrives. All I know is that in the moment she becomes aware of it, I do, too – the news about her son. I can't be sure who brought the word. It might have been an angel of the Lord but I'm more inclined to think it blew in on the soft west wind, landing like a small, dead bird on her aproned lap. She pauses for a moment, the poem forgotten. Her face looks even younger; it wears the frightened, uncertain expression of a young woman who isn't sure what she should do. Then, finally and silently, she climbs down from the wall and crosses the grass between the graves, back to the place where she and my father are buried.

Only when she gets there do I see my father. He, too, is a young man, in his mid-thirties. He is laying a table for the evening meal, a tablecloth – white and shining – flaps gently in the twilight breeze. He is singing softly, sweetly but I can't clearly hear his song and nor can I hear the words my mother speaks to him but I know, by the way his expression changes, by the way his voice falls silent, that she has told him their eldest child is dead. They stand together for a moment and I know the lives ahead of them and behind them are one – the as yet unborn boy's life, the doctor's life, their son's life – and that they are broken-hearted. And I'm broken-hearted for them. And then my father does something unexpected. He lays another place at the table, pulls up another chair and they sit and wait for their son to come and join them.

I wake and feel a sense of hope, a sense that everything will, in time, be well, filled with compassion and with peace.

Brother Ghost

Do you remember the last time the three of us were together – father, son and brother ghost? An autumn evening in our father's room in the hospital and while we were chatting a woman wandered in, a patient. It wasn't immediately obvious that she was suffering from dementia.

She looked at our father and berated him for being in bed, telling him he was suffering from *nothing more than a sore throat and a touch of arthritis*. And, furthermore, he should be out working and not skiving off. *Malingering* was the word she used.

He allowed her to finish her tirade before, politely asking: 'And what precisely, madam, are your medical qualifications?'

The woman beat a hasty retreat and the three of us laughed together.

Do you remember those moments or has the gift of memory deserted you?

Son

Often, at the most unexpected times, Jarlath crossed my mind and I'd wonder about what it means to be brothers but, since his death, there's hardly a day when I don't think about him and about us and about what being a brother means now. And nothing important has changed, none of the beauty, none of the closeness, none of the love has disappeared or dissipated.

When he was alive, I generally knew where he was – Cary, North Carolina or at the beach house in Emerald Isle or, from time to time, here with us. But now I have no idea at all of his whereabouts. His ashes are in Cary and Castledermot – bilocation at last. But his spirit, his soul, the person he was and is, is nowhere and everywhere. He lives in conversations and photographs and thoughts.

Sometimes I imagine him in some heaven of his own believing, and sometimes I visualise him walking the warm beaches of North Carolina, paddling in the balmy waters of the Atlantic, and sometimes I picture him just beyond the light, out there on the periphery of life and that's probably where he felt most at home. I think we shared that inability to be at the heart of any society in which we lived. Jarlath could be the heart and soul of the party, as can I, but his natural home, and mine, is out there on the edge, watching and recording. Maybe that's why he turned to photography when gynaecology lost its allure, maybe he'd found his place in the world, looking and chronicling. And maybe that's why I write – to see what I can see and to record and pack all the bits and pieces into the shapes and the boxes that make poems and stories and books. Wouldn't it have been something to have worked together on a book – his pictures, my words? He did suggest it once.

Weaving its way through these memories is the weft of grief that snarls itself, like a ripped plastic bag in a tree. I think of his body in the Apex funeral home, the pallid corpse of a stranger and I can hardly bear to remember. I'm reminded of Constance's words in Shakespeare's *King John*:

Grief fills the room up of my absent child,
Lies in his bed, walks up and down with me,
Puts on his pretty looks, repeats his words,
Remembers me of all his gracious parts,
Stuffs out his vacant garments with his form;
Then, have I reason to be fond of grief.

I know where to look for him and yet I have no idea where he is. I recall my gentle, classmate Liam Dunne, who died when he was nine, and how, in the days after his burial, I'd look in the wardrobe, search beneath the beds in the lads' rooms before I went to sleep. I had a dread and yet a kind of dark hope that I might find Liam there, that death might not be the great sundering I imagined it to be, that there might be some coming back.

And so it was and so it is with Jarlath. There are days when he is gone beyond communication, beyond hope, and there are other days when he is that ostracised figure living on the edge of town, like Pete Seeger's *Abiyoyo*, happy in his isolation, dignified in his response, content in his aloneness. And on those days I firmly believe I'll walk around some corner, peer more closely into some darkness and there he'll be, with that same sardonic smile as ever, waiting for me with a look that says: *Where have you been, brother? I've been waiting here for you all these years*.

I had a vision, as a child, of how our lives would be and I carried that vision into adulthood and my brother never let me down. He was the repairer, the carer. I remember him swinging me high in his arms but I never, not for a moment, feared he would drop me. I trusted his love and I trusted his wisdom. But what is a vision but a dream and what is a dream but a powerful surge that brings experience in sleep, and anger or disappointment on waking?

I have spent much of my life running but when I ran he was at my shoulder, urging caution, pointing out the pitfalls, looking out for me or, at the very least, just there and, often, his being there was enough. But in the last nineteen years I've been running alone.

Occasionally, I catch a glimpse of a shadow which might be him or might simply be a silhouette of memory.

And now, when it's too late to expect an answer, I ask him if he has even the slightest notion about the purpose of our lives. He always had an answer. It might be a charming piece of fabrication but it would be delivered with style and conviction, with love and carefulness. Now there is no answer, just a chilling silence.

I imagine us driving through North Carolina again, those small towns and scattered homesteads; the long, deserted main streets; the diners with their endless cups of coffee and their mountainous stacks of pancakes; the empty phone boxes, their doors blowing open and shut in the warm summer wind; red clouds of dust as we drive away; a last glance in the wing mirror, a last look and then we're gone.

But now there's no looking back unless, like Lot's unnamed wife, I want to be turned to a pillar of salt or ash or anguish. Yet, I do look back and I look forward and always, in the dusk, there's the brother I lost. Sometimes, I imagine I see him on the edge of a forest or there, between the headstones, at the other end of Coltstown cemetery. But then I wonder: would I recognise him if I met him? Imagine meeting and not knowing each other, passing without recognition. Imagine the cruelty in that.

Father

Another evening in summer but this one is drawn from the mind's eye. I had always visualised the burials happening in the ashy light of dawn but why not on a summer evening, the end of a long and futile day of labour for my mother and now my father begins, again, the harrowing task of wrapping an unmoving, lifeless infant in a pillow case, placing it in a small wooden box, carrying it through the wash of dusky birdsong to the wild patch at the end of his tilled garden.

And, later still, he will lean wearily on the handle of a spade that is angled in the ground beside a small mound of earth. I stand at the top of the garden, in the deep shadow of the shed, and watch. It is so unusual to see him in that position – not working, absorbed in the task he has just completed, that of burying another of his children.

Brother Ghost

The thing I miss most is your laughter.

Son

Sometimes, we become the people our parents make of us. But, always, we become the people we make of ourselves. And, occasionally, we learn to recognise the uncertainty and frailty in our parents' lives, that same frailty we carry within ourselves. And then, if we're lucky, we venture down the road of understanding and mercy.

Acknowledgements: the author wishes to acknowledge the financial assistance of the Arts Council/ An Comhairle Ealaoin in the writing of this memoir.

Thanks to Dolores MacKenna; Clare MacKenna and Holly MacKenna Graffagnini.

Thank you Krista Detor for permission to quote from *Icarus*.

And thank you to Valerie Byrne, Faye Tucker and Mark Turner.

Other titles from The Harvest Press

The Winter Dress – Angela Keogh

A beautifully written and deeply moving novel set during the Black Death.

Rich and complex…The Winter Dress lingers long after the last page – The Irish Times

We Say We Will – Martha Woodcock

A gentle and poignant first collection of poems.

Martha Woodcock is our evoker…She pays attention to the things we forget. Her insightful telling makes small things resonate – Rita Ann Higgins

The Forgotten – Gerard Whelan

The story of the men and women from one parish who served in the Great War.

Neither a eulogy nor an apology…. A powerful evocation. The Irish Times

The Column I Never Wrote – John Masterson

An honest and heart-rending story of teenage love and duplicity and how the events of one summer have thrown a shadow across the author's life.

A slim book, full of fascinating and fertile ideas – explorations of memory, of identity, of psychological suffering, of the stories we tell ourselves and the ways those stories can affect what we choose to do and be – Sunday Independent

***I Knew This Place* – John MacKenna**

A collection of radio essays spanning fifteen years of contributions to the RTE Radio 1 programme Sunday Miscellany.

If I Knew This Place was twice or even three times as long, the reader would still be left yearning for more, as this one was – The Irish Times

***Nothing to be done* – Dermot O'Sullivan**

A gentle remembering of loss, of greater loss and of love. A beautiful testament to youth and maturity.

A heart-breaking memoir – Limerick Leader

Printed in Great Britain
by Amazon

49235661R10119